To: Ladelle
From
Jhn T. Rundles
4/16/98
Carl in Bakersfield, CA

Cooking Naturally
for
Pleasure and Health

Cooking Naturally

for Pleasure and Health

by Gail C. Watson

FALKYNOR BOOKS
Davie, Florida

Cover design by Gail C. Watson
Illustrations by Gail C. Watson and Dover Publications

Copyright© 1982 by Gail C. Watson.
Published by Falkynor Books, Davie, FL
Library of Congress catalog card number:

ISBN: 0-916878-16-3

All rights reserved, which include the right
to reproduce this book or portions thereof in
any form whatsoever. For information, address
Falkynor Books, P.O. Box 290057, Davie, FL 33314.

Library of Congress cataloging and publication data:
Watson, Gail, 1946-
    Cooking Naturally for Pleasure and Health
    Bibliography p. 239

Printed in the U.S.A.

10 9 8 7 6 5 4 3 2

With love and gratitude, this book is dedicated to Michael and the burning of starvation karma;

And to Bhagavan Sri Sathya Sai Baba ...

> "If you sincerely, unhesitatingly, constantly, gladly, lovingly, offer all your skill and strength to the service of others, God will melt and move and manifest Himself in you, before you, with spontaneous grace."

Other titles containing recipes by this author:

* A Way of Eating for Pleasure and Health
* Five Minutes to Fitness with Acugenics
* How to Beat Stress with Acugenics
* How to Lose Weight Easily with Acugenics
* How to Relieve Arthritis with Acugenics

Any of these books may be purchased through your local bookstore, health food store or directly from the publisher.

                        Falkynor Books
                Post Office Box 290057
                Davie, Florida   33314

Acknowledgments

The author wishes to thank and gratefully acknowledge the help and assistance of many members and friends of The G-Jo Institute. She is lovingly indebted to Andrea Holly Gold for her care-full editing, recipe testing and enthusiastic assistance. She is especially grateful to:

* Laurie Blate
* Michael Blate
* Al Fon
* Aude Franks
* Dick Knierim
* Sandy Pasquale
* B R Rock
* Diane Ruby
* Barbara Sisson
* Jimmy Sullivan
* Sharon Tufaro
* Polyana Watson
* Peggy Wells

For further information about the format and design of this book, please see the colophon (located on p. 242).

What Is The G-Jo Institute

The G-Jo Institute is a not-for-profit natural health research and educational organization. It was informally organized in 1976 and incorporated in 1982. Its purpose is the dissemination of drugless "self-health" techniques.

G-Jo is a simplified form of acupuncture without needles (or "acupressure"). However, the scope of the G-Jo Institute has expanded far beyond its original purpose of the sharing of simple acupressure techniques.

It is our belief that it is the body-mind — and only the body-mind — which heals itself. For that reason, we now address ourselves to the entire spectrum of how to stimulate the innate self-healing mechanisms within the body-mind with simple, yet effective, self-applied techniques from around the world.

For further information or catalogs about our publications, recordings, workshops and such, send a business-sized, self-addressed stamped envelope to:

THE G-JO INSTITUTE
DIVISION C
POST OFFICE BOX 8060
HOLLYWOOD, FLA. 33024
U.S.A.

Table of Contents

Foreword by Michael Blate xi

Introduction xiii

Glossary xvi

U.S. Measurement Equivalents xxx

Recipes
    Appetizers, Dips and Spreads 1
    Beverages 15
    Breads 27
    Breakfasts 43
    Desserts 57
    Entrees 89
    Grain Side Dishes 129
    Miscellaneous 143
    Salads and Salad Dressings 149
    Sandwich Combinations 173
    Sauces 179
    Soups 197
    Vegetables 215

General Index 231

Bibliography 239

Colophon 242

Foreword

This foreword is, in part, a "thank you" to Gail for the wonderful meals that have evolved preceding and during the creation of this marvelous cookbook. It is also an encouragement to you, the reader, to share the enjoyment of simple and natural foods, combined in easy yet wholesome and delicious ways.

For the beginner — that is, for the person who has, to this point, eaten in the "typical" Western manner — this is a "welcome back" to the way man has eaten for thousands of years (i.e., in a vegetarian manner). The heavy reliance on meat in the average Western diet is of relatively recent origin.

Your return to a primarily or exclusively vegetarian/fruitarian diet (with or without the addition of milk or other non-slaughtered dairy products) is a return to your nutritional roots as a human being. Our digestive systems are best prepared to handle such a diet...and our consciousness as human beings is best raised and expanded with such a "deathless" diet.

We (at The G-Jo Institute) originally embraced vegetarianism for spiritual and moral reasons — not for the "health" and economic benefits that such a way of eating brings — yet we each loved substantial food served in appealing ways. Gail has kept this in mind in her writing...to this I can most pleasurefully attest. In short, the recipes herein will appeal to — and satisfy — the most demanding or cautious palates (vegetarian or not). The discriminating and experienced vegetarian will quickly see the touch of a master chef in the following pages. The beginner will find Gail's recipes easy to prepare yet skillfully combined for satisfying taste and complete nutrition.

An enormous amount of research has preceded this book. In its compilation and production, Gail has tried to walk the "middle path," providing recipes for both "vegans" (those who avoid <u>all</u> animal products, even milk and other non-slaughtered substances), and others on very strict diets, as well as for "lacto-vegetarians." These are people, like ourselves, who object to animal slaughter but who feel that non-slaughtered dairy products are a non-objectionable way of supplementing grains, vegetables and fruits for complete and convenient nutrition. Gail has also thoughtfully included alternatives and many suggestions for those who suffer from allergies to such common substances as gluten (found in many grains, such as wheat, oats, etc.), dairy products and other typical foodstuffs we Westerners consume.

But it is perhaps in the area of sugar and honey — rather, in the <u>lack</u> of these common but harsh sweeteners — where this book shines the most brightly. Gail provides you with a vast selection of satisfying sweets — especially for the person who has avoided sugar and/or honey for three weeks or more (the typical period for completion of "sugar withdrawal"). I, for one, can fully guarantee these desserts and sweets are satisfying (and this is the testament of a comfirmed but ex-"sugar addict").

The person who has made the decision to eat more humanely will clearly see and appreciate the logic of Gail's thought processes. She is gently showing the reader-cum-cook a radiant pathway of personal evolution toward a simpler and more loving way of being — the way of right diet. In that respect, she is a quite trustworthy guide: her dedication to self-enlightenment is... most remarkable. Thus, it is with great pleasure that I introduce you to — and encourage you to enjoy — the following recipes and suggestions for eating.

Michael Blate   Summer, 1982

Introduction

The recipes to follow were created or adapted over the past few years to provide health-full and pleasure-full meals for my family and friends at the G-Jo Institute. It is my wish that they will do the same for you and your loved ones. At the G-Jo Institute, we have found our meals to be more health- and pleasureful when we keep the following in mind:

1. If the ingredients used are fresh and of the highest available quality ...

2. If the food is prepared and served consciously with love and concern for those who will consume it ...

3. If the food is prepared with an awareness of balancing color (green, yellow, red, brown and white), texture (rough, smooth, crunchy, soft), temperature (hot-cold, warm-cool) and taste (sweet, sour, bitter, salty, pungent) ...

4. If the food is served in a peaceful, congenial and attractive setting with gently uplifting music, fresh flowers, earth-tone colored dishes and table coverings and very little or at least quiet conversation ...

5. If the food is eaten with an attitude of appreciation, pleasure and love ...

then the food cannot help but provide physical and spiritual nourishment.

For a more complete understanding of our philosophy of eating, please see A WAY OF EATING FOR PLEASURE AND HEALTH (by Michael Blate) available through the G-Jo Institute.

It cannot be said that preparing a nutritionally balanced, attractive and good-tasting vegetarian meal takes less time or energy than fixing the average American meal. Today, with the availability of convenience foods, preparing fresh vegetables, soups, sauces, desserts, etc. — instead of using canned, frozen or freeze-dried products — seems like a lot of work. But there are a few important kitchen helpers which I recommend that cut preparation time dramatically (some of which, although they may be expensive initial investments, will save more than they cost in time and energy in the first few weeks of use alone):

1. Food processor: A good one slices, grates, chops and blends — and in seconds, rather than minutes or hours. It comes with adjustable speeds and interchangeable blades. Not only does the food processor make cooking easier and more fun, it brings gourmet cooking within the reach of beginning cooks — it's like a second pair of hands.

2. Stainless steel skillets and sauce pans: I use the heavy stainless steel pots with a copper base for less metal contamination of the food.

3. Pressure cooker: A stainless steel one, if possible, can save hours of cooking time for beans, grains, soups and stews.

4. Wok: Whether you choose an electric or stove top wok, this handy Chinese cooking pot allows people on low-calorie, low-cholesterol diets to steam or stir-fry their meals with little or no oil.

5. Juicer: For those who enjoy the taste of fresh vegetables and fruit juices there are several types of electric and hand-operated juicers available. Your local natural food store should be able to demonstrate the different features of each to help you decide what will best suit your needs.

6. Crockpot or slow cooker: The person working 9-5 will find the crockpot to be an enormous help. Beans, grains, stews, one-dish meals can go into the pot at breakfast, simmer very slowly and safely, requiring very little electricity, and be ready to serve when you get home at night.

7. Steamer basket: Steaming vegetables in a small, stainless steel collapsible steamer basket allows them to retain more of their color, flavor and nutritional value than the boiling method. The baskets are very inexpensive and available in natural food stores, department stores and grocery stores.

8. In addition to the standard kitchen tools and utensils, a few smaller "indispensible" items include a good set of sharp knives, a stainless steel wire whisk, small and large mesh strainers, a pepper mill, a sturdy garlic press, a pastry blender and wooden spoons of all sizes.

Remember, good quality lasts and the time you save and the pleasure you derive from using quality "helpers" will show in the food you prepare and your family's physical, emotional and spiritual good health.

xvi

Glossary

BAKING POWDER: Low-sodium, cereal-free baking powder is available for those on special diets but is probably healthier for everyone than using the aluminium and sodium compounds found in regular baking powder. It is usually found in natural food stores. (Use 1 1/2 times the required amount of regular baking powder.)

BEANS (see Index — beans; lentils; peas): The legume family is composed of beans, peas and lentils, which are inexpensive, useful sources of protein, especially when combined with grains and seeds.

CAROB POWDER: Also called St. John's bread, carob powder is ground from the pods of the carob tree. It is naturally sweet, rich in minerals and low in calories and fat. It contains none of the stimulants of chocolate, but has a similar taste. Carob powder can be purchased in its natural state or toasted for a fuller, nutty flavor and is used in place of chocolate or cocoa (3 Tbsp. carob plus 2 Tbsp. water or milk = 1 square chocolate).

CHEESE, RENNETLESS: Many imported and traditional cheeses contain rennet, a coagulant made from the stomach linings of young calves and are, therefore undesirable to vegetarians. Many domestic, mass-produced cheeses (e.g., Cheddar, Jack, muenster, Swiss, etc.) are now made with a vegetable coagulant. Most natural food stores carry rennetless cheeses and some brands are salt-free. Most grocery stores carry a variety of cheeses for low-fat, low-cholesterol and low-calorie diets, but check the labels carefully.

DAIRY SUBSTITUTES (also see Index): Soy products and/or nuts can be used to make substitutes for milk and many other dairy products (e.g., butter, cream, cream cheese, ricotta cheese, sour cream, etc.) These offer welcome options to those with allergies to dairy products.

EGG REPLACER: Natural food stores carry an egg replacer made mainly of potato starch and tapioca flour which we use as a substitute for eggs when a nut butter, oatmeal or other binders can not be appropriately used. For baking purposes, 2 Tbsp. lecithin granules, 1 tsp. arrowroot flour and 2 Tbsp. water = 1 egg.

FLOURS: The following stone-ground, whole-grain flours are available in most natural food stores: Buckwheat; cornmeal; brown rice; rye; soybean; triticale; whole wheat pastry; and whole wheat. We grind millet into flour ourselves and buy Gram (chickpea) flour from an Indian grocery.

FRUIT, DRIED: Unsweetened, unsulphured dried fruits are drier than commercial brands but have more flavor. They can be soaked in water to soften, reserving the liquid to use as a natural syrup. Unsulphured apples, apricots, cherries, dates, figs, peaches, pears, pineapple, prunes, raisins or mixed fruits are available at natural food stores.

FRUIT JUICE CONCENTRATES: Especially for people on low-sugar diets, fruit juice concentrates, used sparingly, open the door to a multitude of foods usually "off limits." Orange, apple and grape concentrates are available in frozen form in the grocery store. A larger variety comes in bottled form at natural food stores (black cherry, apricot, cranberry, strawberry, etc.) Fruit juice concentrate can be used in place of sugar, honey or any sweetener, but remember: It is a very concentrated form of fruit sugar — use accordingly.

GRAINS (see Index — Grains) A grain is the seed/fruit of a member of the cereal-grass family. Grains provide a high quality source of protein for over half of the world's population and when combined with milk products or legumes, the amount of usable protein greatly increases. The following grains are easily available in the grocery store or natural food store:

    BARLEY: Hulled barley is a darker and less processed grain than the whiter "pearled" barley, and therefore contains more nutritional value. Hulled barley is available in most natural food stores and pearled barley can usually be found in a grocery store. Both are used mainly in soups and casseroles. Barley is also ground into grits and cooked as a cereal.

    BROWN RICE: Rice is the staple food for over half of the world's population and, in our experience, is the most suitable energy-balancing grain for the human body. Rice that has been husked but not polished like white rice is called brown rice. Because it is less processed, it retains more protein and nutritive value. The long grain variety is usually available in grocery stores and cooks up light and fluffy. The short grain variety is more glutenous, therefore more moist when cooked. Both are usually available at natural food stores and have a wonderful, full-bodied flavor.

BUCKWHEAT: Not really a grain, buckwheat is the fruit of a plant classified with acorns, chestnuts, amaranth, chia and water chestnuts. It is known for its warming properties in cold weather. It can be roasted (see Kasha) to bring out the flavor, or ground into a buckwheat cereal. Buckwheat is used in casseroles, as a cereal or made into patties (Japanese Soba Gaki). It is also ground into flour to use in pancakes, waffles or muffins. Natural food stores usually carry buckwheat and buckwheat flour while soba noodles and 100% buckwheat spaghetti are available at Oriental groceries.

BULGUR (bulghur, bulgar, burghul): Often used interchangeably with cracked wheat, bulgur is actually whole grain wheat that has been parboiled, dried and cracked. It can be soaked and used raw in salads (tabouli) or cooked as a cereal or grain side dish.

CORN: Used as vegetable and grain, corn commonly comes in two colors — the white corn variety has a more subtle flavor; the yellow is higher in vitamin A and has a stronger flavor. Yellow corn is also higher in protein value but both varieties combine well with beans to increase the usable protein. Corn of either color is ground into cornmeal and used in breads, muffins, hoe cakes and waffles.

KASHA: Roasted buckwheat groats, or kasha, is a Russian-Eurasian staple food. Kasha can be bought in fine, medium, coarse or whole groat textures. It has a strong nutty flavor and is also good mixed with brown rice for a cereal or casserole.

MILLET: Referred to as "poor man's rice," millet is a tiny, round, light yellow grain with a subtle sweet taste. It is sometimes used in place of rice and mixes well with other grains. It is often used in soups, cereals, and stuffings.

OATS: Although rolled oats (oatmeal) are more commonly used, whole hulled oats are occasionally used as a cereal or in soups. Oatmeal is often used in waffles, cookies, meatless loaves, as a binder or leavening agent.

RYE: Rye is a hearty grain used more commonly today in flaked, grit or flour form. As a flour, it is usually combined with wheat to make breads while whole rye is used in casseroles or stews.

TRITICALE: Originally a cross between Durham wheat, hard red winter wheat and rye, triticale is now a grain breeding variety in its own right. It contains a better balanced protein than wheat or rye alone and has a slightly sweet taste. It can be sprouted, flaked or used whole in casseroles, cereals, cookies, loaves and patties, or ground to a flour and used with wheat in breads.

WHEAT, CRACKED: Cracked wheat is whole grain wheat that has been crushed. It is often used interchangeably with bulgur in recipes, but unlike bulgur, it must be cooked before eaten.

WHOLE WHEAT: Wheat is probably the most commonly used grain in the U.S. (although usually as a highly processed flour). Whole wheatberries can be cooked and eaten as a cereal or used in casseroles, etc. or they can be flaked, cracked, parboiled ("bulgur") or ground into a flour.

HERBS: Fresh herbs grown at home or dried herbs from the store bestow a touch of elegance on the simplest of dishes. Besides having very beneficial healing properties for many health problems (see the G-Jo Institute's MANUAL OF MEDICINAL HERBS), herbs are very effective replacements for salt in low-sodium diets. Some suggestions for herb or spice substitutions for salt are offered in the American Heart Association's COOKING WITHOUT YOUR SALT SHAKER for the following vegetables:

Asparagus: Garlic, lemon juice, onion, vinegar.
Corn: Green pepper, pimento, fresh tomato.
Cucumbers: Chives, dill, garlic, vinegar.
Green Beans: Dill, lemon juice, marjoram, nutmeg, pimento.
Greens: Onion, pepper, vinegar.
Peas: Green pepper, mint, fresh mushrooms, onion, parsley.
Potatoes: Green pepper, mace, onion, paprika, parsley.
Rice: Chives, green pepper, onion, pimento, saffron.
Squash: Sweetener, cinnamon, ginger, mace, nutmeg, onion.
Tomatoes: Basil, marjoram, onion, oregano.
Soups: A pinch of dry mustard powder in bean soup; allspice, a small amount of vinegar or a dash of sweetener in vegetable soup; peppercorns in skim milk chowders; bay leaf and parsley in pea soups.

HERB SEASONING SALT: Several combinations of
dried herbs, vegetables and sea salt are available
in natural food stores. These combinations provide
a tasty, less salty vegetarian seasoning for many
salt-conscious people. Be sure to read the labels
for substances you might not wish to consume or to
which you may be allergic.

LIQUID SOY PROTEIN: An all-vegetable, concentrated
liquid aminos made from soybeans is available in
natural food stores. We often use it in place of
salt or tamari because of its gentle flavor.

MISO (mee-zo): Miso is a paste made from fermented
soybeans. It is high in protein, natural enzymes, B
vitamins (including B_{12})...and it aids digestion (as
does yogurt). It does contain about 12% salt but it
takes less to bring out the flavor of foods (1 Tbsp.
miso = 1/2 tsp. salt). Miso is used as a seasoning for
soups, sauces, dips and salad dressings, but it should
not be boiled or the enzymes and digestive mico-
organisms are destroyed. It is found in natural food
stores or Oriental groceries and comes in a variety of
flavors and colors:

> Hacho miso (soybeans, water and salt);
> Mugi (barley, soybeans, water and salt);
> Kome, red miso (rice, soybeans, water and salt);
> Brown rice, brown miso — strong and hearty —
> (brown rice, soybeans, water and salt);
> White miso — very mild and slightly sweet —
> (rice, soybeans, water and salt.)

NUTS: Nuts are a highly concentrated food — a good
source of protein and unsaturated fat. They are
more easily digested when chewed well and eaten
fresh and raw. The following varieties are found
at most natural food stores and/or grocery stores:

Almonds; black walnuts; Brazil nuts; cashews; chestnuts; coconuts; macadamias; pecans; peanuts (actually a legume); pine nuts; pistachios; etc.

NUT BUTTERS (see individual nuts in the Index for recipes): Nuts, especially almonds, cashews and peapeanuts, are easily ground into a butter consistency and are a good source of protein and unrefined, unsaturated fats. Nut butters have a variety of uses: as a spread on crackers or sandwiches; in sauces or dressings; as a thickener, binder, and source of fat in loaves and casseroles.

NUT MILKS & CREAMS (see Index for recipes): Sweet nuts, especially almonds and cashews, can be ground into a powder, diluted with water and seasoned to make delicious milk and cream substitutes.

OILS: Two types of oil may be purchased — unrefined (unsaturated) and refined (unsaturated or saturated). We recommend unrefined and unsaturated oils for general use with only occasional use of saturated oils (butter or soy margarine). To obtain unrefined oils, seeds, grains, nuts, etc., are cold-pressed or lightly heated, then pressed, to release the oils. Either way, no chemicals are used for the extraction process; no refining, bleaching or deodorizing is done. Unrefined oils stay liquid at room temperature; there may be some sediment and the odors are generally stronger but the nutritional value is much higher than in refined or saturated oils.

Combining or using a variety of unrefined oils also increases their nutritional value. These oils, as a general rule, should not be heated over 350°F. (or to the point of smoking) as the heat causes toxic chemical changes. Safflower and peanut oils are the exception and may be used for deep-frying at 375-400°F.

Most natural food stores sell unrefined corn germ, olive, peanut, soy, safflower, sesame and sunflower oils. Whenever possible, buy the cold-pressed for your salad dressings and cooking needs. Some foods high in unsaturated fats include avocados, olives, nuts and seeds. Saturated fats that remain solid at room temperatures include butter, soy margarine and vegetable shortening; use in moderation.

OLIVES: Naturally preserved and seasoned olives are available at natural food stores, but the salt content is still relatively high — use cautiously.

PASTA: While most pastas are made of refined wheat, other whole and processed grains are sometimes ground into flour and used (frequently in combination with bean or vegetable flours) to make the following pastas:
    100% buckwheat spaghetti (imported from Japan);
    100% rice spaghetti and noodles (imported from China);
    Bean and potato flour threads (imported from China);
    Combination semolina, soy and Jerusalem artichoke flour spaghetti, noodles, macaroni and lasagna (from natural food stores);
    100% corn spaghetti and macaroni (from natural food stores);
    Whole wheat spaghetti, noodles, macaroni and lasagna (from natural food stores).

POWDERED VEGETABLE BROTH: Dehydrated vegetables and sea salt are ground to a fine powder and often fortified with nutritional yeast to make a dry vegetable broth or bouillon. Several brands are available, which can be mixed with water for a quick vegetable stock base for cooking beans, grains, sauces or soups.

PROTEIN POWDER, UNSWEETENED: Read the labels of different powdered protein supplements carefully to find one that is unsweetened and free of slaughtered animal products. A balanced diet supplies plenty of protein, but in times of stress or extra activity, the temporary use of supplements mixed into beverages can provide that needed extra boost.

SALT, SEA SALT (also see Herb Seasoning Salt, Herbs): Unrefined sea salt that has been solar-evaporated, then gently dried, is usually chemical- and sugar-free and is high in natural trace minerals. It is available in natural food stores, but remember to use salt or any high-sodium products in moderation.

SEA VEGETABLES: The vegetables harvested from the ocean are very rich in vitamins and minerals. They are generally unfamilar to Americans but can be cooked like regular greens, used in soups, salads, appetizers, etc., or powdered for a salt substitute (kelp). The most common are kelp, nori, dulse and wakame; these and others can be found at natural food stores or Oriental groceries.

SEEDS: High in protein, unsaturated fats, vitamins and minerals, seeds are most nutritious when eaten raw. They make a great snack alone or combined with nuts and dried fruit or used as a spread, when ground in with a nut butter. Seeds add nutrition, flavor and texture to salads, casseroles, loaves and soups. They need to be chewed well, ground or chopped (see Gomasio) for easier digestibility. The most commonly used seeds include sesame, sunflower and pumpkin and can be found raw or toasted and salted or unsalted in natural food stores.

SPROUTS: Sprouting seeds, beans and grains greatly increases their nutritional value and digestibility. Use organically grown seeds if possible and only those sold for growing (planting seeds are often mixed well with fungicides and pesticides). The most commonly sprouted seeds are alfalfa, mung beans, lentils and wheat, but many more are available at natural foods stores. Sprouts are delicious alone, in salads and sandwiches or mixed into casseroles, etc. The fresher they are when eaten, the more the nutritional value.

SWEETENERS: There are many "harsh" sweeteners available (including white sugar, raw sugar, honey, molasses and fructose) that we have found to "imbalance" the delicate blood sugar levels of many people. Fresh and dried fruit, maple syrup (in moderation), fruit juice concentrates, rice and barley syrup, etc., seem to be more slowly broken down into glucose and absorbed into the blood, therefore not as disturbing as the "harsh" sweets.

All too often, beginning (and even experienced) vegetarians make the mistake of failing to drastically reduce (and preferably avoid) the intake of harsh sweets (or alcohol) that meat-eaters need to "neutralize" the extreme biochemical effects caused by slaughtered foods. However, failing to reduce the use of harsh sweets — including alcohol — quickly results in emotional depression, often lethargy and a tendency toward anger and short-temperedness. This is especially true for people who go immediately into a fruitarian (fruit-based) diet without first spending several years "weaning" themselves from slaughtered products by following a grain-based diet.

TAHINI (also see Index): Tahini is made of hulled sesame seeds ground into a butter. It is commonly used in the Middle East and is very nutritious and easily digested. It is milder in flavor and a little lower in mineral content than sesame butter which is made from unhulled sesame seeds. Tahini is used in salad dressings, loaves, burgers, casseroles and as a thickener or binder.

TAMARI: Tamari is a naturally fermented soy sauce made from soybeans, sea salt, water and sometimes wheat. It is used in place of salt but is still relatively high in sodium. It adds extra flavor and color to sauces, gravies, soups, grains, etc. It is especially good in stir-fried dishes.

THICKENING AGENTS (see Index — listed individually): The following substances can be used in a variety of recipes because of their unique coagulating properties:

    AGAR-AGAR: A clear, tasteless vegetarian replacement for animal gelatin, agar-agar is made from sea algae and comes in granulated, flaked and bar form (called Kantan).

    2 Tbsp. gelatin = 1 Tbsp. granulated agar
    1 Tbsp. granulated agar = 2 Tbsp. flaked agar, each will gel 3 cups liquid
    1 Kantan bar (1/4 oz.) will gel 1 1/3 cups liquid

    ARROWROOT: Made from the root of a tropical plant, arrowroot is high in minerals and easily digested. It is used mainly in puddings, sauces, etc. (It must be dissolved in cold liquid before adding to heated sauces; then simmered only a minute or so.)

Sauces using arrowroot should not be reheated as its thickening properties break down.

FLOUR: Any whole-grain flour can be used to make a white sauce or roux (see recipes) to thicken sauces, gravies, soups, etc.

STARCHES: Cornstarch and potato starch can be used interchangeably with arrowroot to thicken liquids. Potato starch is particularly helpful to those allergic to corn.

TAPIOCA: In addition to their thickening properties, the tropical tapioca granules add a delightful texture to puddings and pies.

TOFU (see Index): The food of a thousand tastes, tofu is a cheese-like soybean curd. It is bland-tasting and absorbs the flavors of the ingredients with which it is cooked. It is an inexpensive protein source containing virtually all of the essential amino acids and is now available at grocery as well as natural food stores. Because of its nutritional value and versatility, it can be served as any course in a meal from appetizer to dessert.

VEGETABLE STOCK: A good base for soups, sauces, etc., can be made in any of the following ways:

1. Save leftover water from steamed or boiled vegetables;
2. Dissolve vegetable broth or vegetable bouillon cubes in water;
3. Make a broth by simmering raw carrots, potatoes, celery, broccoli, cauliflower, etc., in water until tender, then removing (or blending in a food processor or blender and returning to the broth for a thicker stock).

VINEGAR: Vinegar is the end product of the fermentation process and, therefore, people sensitive to sugar and/or alcohol may also be unable to use much of it. Whenever possible, we use more natural and nutritious lemon juice in its place. When the special tanginess of vinegar is necessary, the delicate flavor of a natural rice vinegar or apple cider vinegar is our choice.

U.S. Measurement Equivalents

Pinch	=	less than 1/8 tsp.
3 tsp.	=	1 Tbsp.
2 Tbsp.	=	1 fluid ounce
4 Tbsp.	=	1/4 cup
5 Tbsp. 1 tsp.	=	1/3 cup
8 Tbsp.	=	1/2 cup
1 cup	=	1/2 pint or 8 fluid ounces
2 cups	=	1 pint or 16 fluid ounces
2 pints	=	1 quart
4 quarts	=	1 gallon

Appetizers, Dips and Spreads

Almond Butter, 2
Banana-Date Nut Butter, 2
Cashew Butter, 2
Celery Stuffing, 3
Cheddar Cheese Straws, 3
Cream Cheese Treats, 4
Cucumber-Spinach Dip, 4
Curried Cashew Spread, 5
Date Dip or Stuffing, 6
Fresh Vegetable Platter, 6
Great Northern Bean Spread, 7
Green Chili Dip, 8
Homemade Potato Chips, 8
Hommus, 9
Horseradish Dip, 9
Marinated Mushrooms, 10
Peanut Butter, 10
Toasted Butter Pecans, 11
Tofu-Dill Dip, 11
Tofu-Fruit Dip, 12
Tofu-Pineapple Spread, 12
Tomato Mexicali Dip, 13
Vegetable Garden Dip, 14

ALMOND BUTTER

2 cups blanched almonds
1 Tbsp. oil, optional
Sea salt to taste, optional

Place the almonds in a food processor or grinder and blend to the desired consistency. If oil and salt are to be added, blend in just as the nuts turn into butter. Makes about 1 1/2 cups.

BANANA-DATE NUT BUTTER

1/2 cup chopped pecans or walnuts
1/2 cup pitted dates
1 small banana
1/8 tsp. cinnamon, ginger and/or cardamom

Combine all the ingredients in a food processor and blend until smooth. Refrigerate until ready to serve as a dip or sandwich spread. Makes about 1 1/2 cups.

CASHEW BUTTER

2 cups raw or lightly toasted cashews
1 Tbsp. oil, optional
Sea salt to taste, optional

Place the cashews in a food processor or grinder and blend to the desired consistency. If oil and salt are to be added, blend in just as the nuts turn into butter. Makes about 1 1/2 cups.

CELERY STUFFING

1 cup MOCK or LOW-FAT "CREAM CHEESE" p. 145-6
1/2 cup chopped olives
1 Tbsp. minced sweet red pepper
Celery stalks, cut into 3-inch pieces

Mix the cream cheese and chopped olives together well. Stuff generously into the hollow sides of the celery sticks. Makes at least 1 dozen celery pieces.

CHEDDAR CHEESE STRAWS

1/2 lb. Cheddar cheese, grated
3 Tbsp. soft butter or soy margarine
3/4 cup flour (unbleached, whole wheat, rice, soy, etc.)
1/8 tsp. sea salt
Dash of hot pepper sauce

Combine all of the ingredients and knead into a dough. Makes about 4 dozen.

TO USE IMMEDIATELY: Press the dough through a pastry tube to make 2-inch straws. Bake on a cookie sheet in a preheated oven at 475°F. for about 10 minutes.

TO PREPARE AHEAD: Form the dough into cylindrical rolls, wrap in plastic and place in the freezer. When ready to bake, remove the dough rolls and slice into thin wafers. Follow the baking instructions above.

CREAM CHEESE TREATS

Form MOCK or LOW-FAT "CREAM CHEESE" p. 145-6 into small balls and roll in granola or chopped nuts. Serve as an appetizer or store in the refrigerator for snacks.

CUCUMBER-SPINACH DIP

1 lb. fresh or frozen, chopped spinach
1 large cucumber, sliced
3 green onions with tops, sliced
1/2 cup buttermilk or thinned TOFU
    MAYONNAISE p. 147
1 Tbsp. lemon juice
Pinch of cumin powder
Pinch of garlic powder
Sea salt and pepper to taste

Steam the spinach; drain and reserve the liquid to use as vegetable stock in other recipes. Place the drained spinach in a food processor; add the remaining ingredients and blend until smooth. Chill well and serve with chips, crackers or raw vegetables. Makes about 2 cups.

CURRIED CASHEW SPREAD

2 Tbsp. butter or soy margarine
2 cups cashew pieces
1-2 Tbsp. curry powder
1 1/2 cups vegetable stock
1 cup cooked BROWN RICE p. 132
1 Tbsp. tamari
1/4 tsp. onion powder
1 tsp. sea salt
1 Tbsp. lemon juice
1/4 tsp. cayenne pepper

In a large skillet, melt the butter and sauté the cashews over low heat, until lightly browned. Add the curry powder and continue to cook, stirring continuously, for about 5 minutes. Drain the cashews on a paper towel and allow to cool. In a food processor, blend the cooled nuts into cashew butter. Add the rice and vegetable stock; blend until smooth. Add the remaining ingredients and blend well. Serve as a dip or spread. Makes about 3 cups.

FOR LOW-FAT DIETS:
Toast the cashews without butter and add the curry powder after the nuts are ground into cashew butter.

DATE DIP OR STUFFING

1 cup MOCK or LOW-FAT "CREAM CHEESE" p. 145-6
2 Tbsp. barley malt or maple syrup
1/8 tsp. cinnamon
1/8 tsp. cardamom
1/8 tsp. ginger
2 Tbsp. chopped raisins
2 Tbsp. chopped nuts
2 Tbsp. chopped dates

Mix all the ingredients well and use as a dip for sliced fruit and crackers or stuff into pitted dates. Makes about 1 1/4 cups.

FRESH VEGETABLE PLATTER

Tomato wedges
Sliced cucumbers
Carrot sticks or curls
Celery sticks
Radish flowers
Sliced summer squash
Cauliflower and broccoli
    flowerettes, lightly steamed
Sliced cooked beets
Whole mushrooms
Red and green pepper rings
Any other favorite vegetables

Arrange the vegetables attractively on a large platter, varying color and shape. Serve with a variety of dips p. 1 (TOFU-DILL, CURRIED CASHEW, HOMMUS, ETC.).

GREAT NORTHERN BEAN SPREAD

4 cups cooked Great Northern beans
Vegetable stock, as needed
1/2 sweet red pepper, chopped
2 green onions, chopped
1 stalk celery, chopped
1-2 Tbsp. oil
1/8 tsp. dried or 1/4 tsp. minced fresh basil
1/4 tsp. dried or 1/2 tsp. minced fresh parsley
Garlic powder to taste
Onion powder to taste
1/4 cup liquid soy protein or 2 Tbsp. tamari
1 cup cooked BROWN RICE p. 132

In a food processor or blender, purée half of the beans, adding a little vegetable stock as needed to blend. Meanwhile, in a large skillet, sauté the chopped vegetables in the oil until tender; stir in the herbs and liquid soy protein or tamari. Add the puréed beans, the remaining whole beans and the rice; mix well and simmer until the mixture has thickened into a paste. Chill and serve as a sandwich spread, a dip for crackers or fresh vegetables, or as a stuffing for fresh tomatoes or green peppers. Makes about 4 cups.

GREEN CHILI DIP

1 cup yogurt
1/4 cup TOFU MAYONNAISE p. 147
1/2 tsp. chili powder
2 leaves cilantro (fresh coriander), minced, optional
1 4-oz. can whole green chilies or 4 or 5 roasted fresh green chilies, finely chopped
1/2 cup black olives, pitted and finely chopped
Sea salt or herb seasoning salt to taste

Combine all the ingredients in a small bowl and mix well. Cover and chill for about 1 hour. Garnish with a sprig of fresh cilantro and serve with tortilla chips or raw vegetables. Makes about 2 cups.

HOMEMADE POTATO CHIPS

4 medium potatoes
Ice water
Oil for deep-fryer
Sea salt or herb seasoning salt to taste

Wash the potatoes and slice them paper-thin using a vegetable slicer or food processor. Soak the slices in ice water for about 1 hour; dry thoroughly between paper towels. Drop the chips, a few at a time, into a deep-fryer, preheated to 365°F., for about 3 minutes until golden brown. Shake the basket or stir the chips to separate them as they fry; drain on paper towels and salt as desired. Serves 6.

HOMMUS

3 cups cooked garbanzo beans (chickpeas)
2 cloves garlic, minced
1/3 cup fresh lemon juice
1 tsp. sea salt or to taste
1/2 cup tahini (sesame seed paste)
2 Tbsp. oil
1/3 cup chopped fresh parsley
1/2 cup plain yogurt, optional

Blend all the ingredients in a food processor or blender until smooth and creamy. Serve as a spread for crackers, a filling for pita bread or a dip for a FRESH VEGETABLE PLATTER p. 6. Makes 4 cups.

HORSERADISH DIP

1 cup cooked beets, drained
1 tsp. powdered vegetable broth
2 Tbsp. vegetable stock
1 Tbsp. powdered horseradish
1 tsp. cider or rice vinegar
1/4 tsp. onion powder
1/4 tsp. garlic powder
1/4 tsp. dry mustard
Sea salt to taste

Combine all the ingredients in a blender or food processor and blend until smooth. Serve with crackers, chips, or raw vegetables. Makes about 1 1/4 cups.

MARINATED MUSHROOMS

1 lb. fresh mushrooms
1/4 cup chopped fresh parsley
1/2 cup chopped green onions
FRENCH LEMON DRESSING p. 169

Cut the large mushrooms in half and leave the small ones whole. Place in a mixing bowl with the parsley and green onions; cover with FRENCH LEMON DRESSING or marinade of choice and chill at least 1 hour. Serve on a bed of watercress or lettuce and provide toothpicks or hors d'oeuvre forks. Serves 8.

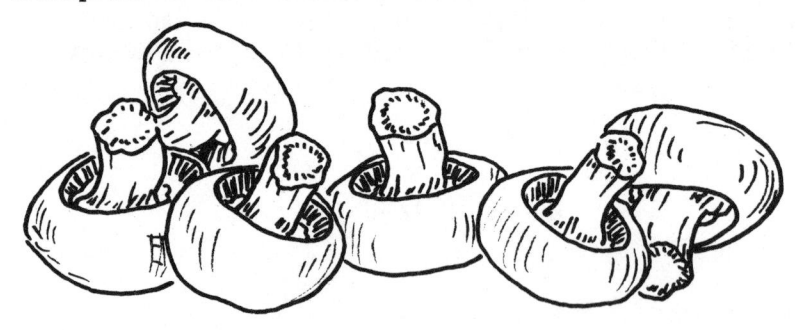

PEANUT BUTTER

2 cups raw or lightly toasted peanuts
1 Tbsp. oil, optional
Sea salt to taste, optional

Place the peanuts in a food processor or grinder and process to the desired consistency. If oil and salt are to be added, blend in just as the nuts turn into butter. Makes about 1 1/2 cups.

TOASTED BUTTER PECANS

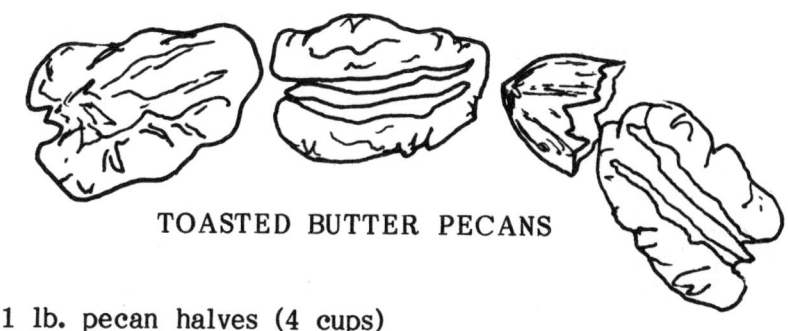

1 lb. pecan halves (4 cups)
1/2 tsp. sea salt or herb seasoning salt
4 Tbsp. butter or soy margarine, optional

Spread the pecans evenly on a cookie sheet. Sprinkle lightly with salt and dot with butter. Bake at 325°F. for about 20 minutes or until browned, turning frequently. Cool and serve. Makes 4 cups.

TOFU-DILL DIP

1 lb. tofu
2 Tbsp. lemon juice
2 Tbsp. oil
1/2 tsp. sea salt
1/2-1 tsp. dill weed or seeds
2 Tbsp. chopped fresh parsley
Pinch of garlic powder

Drop the tofu into boiling water for 2-3 minutes to freshen; drain and blend with the remaining ingredients in a food processor or blender until smooth and creamy. Serve chilled with cut vegetables, chips or crackers. Makes 2 cups.

TOFU-FRUIT DIP

1/2 lb. tofu
1/2 cup apple juice
1 Tbsp. lemon juice
1/8 tsp. cinnamon
1/8 tsp. cardamom
1/8 tsp. ginger
Pinch of sea salt
2 Tbsp. chopped raisins
2 Tbsp. chopped nuts
2 Tbsp. chopped dates
2 Tbsp. chopped dried apples or apricots

Soak the dried apples or apricots in boiling water for 20 minutes; drain and set aside. Drop the tofu into boiling water for 2-3 minutes to freshen; drain and blend in a food processor with the juices and spices, until smooth. Add the apples or apricots and the remaining ingredients to the tofu mixture; blend well, adding more apple juice as needed to thin. Chill and garnish with fresh mint; serve with fresh fruit slices or crackers. Makes about 2 cups.

TOFU-PINEAPPLE SPREAD

1/2 lb. tofu
1/2 cup chopped dried pineapple
1/4 cup pineapple juice
1/4 cup orange juice concentrate
1/4 cup black walnuts, chopped
Pinch of sea salt

Continued next page...

Drop the tofu into boiling water and boil for 2-3 minutes. Drain and blend with the remaining ingredients in a blender or food processor until smooth. Serve chilled with fresh fruit slices or crackers. Makes 2 cups.

TOMATO MEXICALI DIP

1 small onion, thinly sliced
4 lb. peeled tomatoes, chopped
1 clove garlic, minced
1/8 tsp. cardamom seeds or powder
1/2-1 tsp. ground cumin
1 bay leaf
Sea salt and pepper to taste
1 Tbsp. lemon juice or cider or rice vinegar
1 Tbsp. apple juice concentrate
A dash of hot pepper sauce
Chili powder or cayenne pepper to taste
Chopped fresh parsley

In a large skillet, heat a little oil and sauté the onion until tender. Add the tomatoes, garlic, cardamom seeds, cumin, bay leaf, salt and pepper. Simmer, stirring occasionally, for about 30 minutes until the liquid evaporates and the mixture thickens. Strain the purée into a saucepan, to remove the seeds and bay leaf. Add the lemon juice or vinegar, apple juice concentrate, hot sauce and chili powder; bring to a boil, adjust the seasoning to taste and simmer the mixture for a few more minutes. Pour into a serving bowl, sprinkle with chopped parsley and serve hot with crackers or chips. Makes about 3 cups.

VEGETABLE GARDEN DIP

1 cup MOCK or LOW-FAT "SOUR CREAM" p. 145-6
1/4 cup finely chopped radishes
1/4 cup finely chopped green onions
1/4 cup finely chopped green pepper
1/4 cup finely chopped sweet red pepper
1/4 cup finely chopped cucumber
1 clove garlic, minced
1/2-1 tsp. sea salt
1/8 tsp. ground white pepper
2 tsp. apple juice concentrate, optional

Combine all the ingredients in a small bowl and mix well. Chill and garnish with a sprinkle of paprika or a sprig of fresh parsley. Serve with crackers or a FRESH VEGETABLE PLATTER p. 6. Makes 2 cups.

Beverages

Almond Milk, 16
Apple Milk, 16
Cantaloupe Water, 17
Cashew Milk, 17
Fig Lassi, 18
Fizzy Fruit Punch, 18
Fresh Fruit Smoothies, 19-21
Fruit Soda, 22
Mystery Milk, 23
Nut Milk, 23
Raw Vegie Juices, 24-25
Spiced Apple Cider, 26
Sweet Lassi, 26

ALMOND MILK (also see NUT MILK p. 23)

1 1/2 cups raw almonds
3 cups water
1 Tbsp. oil, optional
1 Tbsp. sweetener (fruit juice concentrate, maple syrup or barley malt), optional
1/8 tsp. sea salt, optional

Blanch the almonds by dropping them into boiling water. After a minute or so the skins will slip off in your fingertips. Place the blanched almonds in a food processor or blender and chop to a fine meal. Add the water (and optional ingredients) and blend again for about 3 minutes or until smooth. Strain if desired, but the tiny pieces that remain make a nice crunchy texture in cereals and sauces. Makes 1 quart.

APPLE MILK

2 cups NUT MILK p. 23
3 or 4 apples, washed and quartered
Apple juice concentrate, optional
Cinnamon to taste

Place the NUT MILK and apples in a food processor or blender and process until smooth. A little apple juice concentrate and/or cinnamon may be added to sweeten, if desired. Serve as a beverage or over cereals. Makes about 3 cups.

CANTALOUPE WATER

2 ripe cantaloupes
1-1 1/2 cups cold water
1/4 cup sweetener (fruit juice concentrate, rice syrup, barley malt, maple syrup, etc.), optional
10 ice cubes

Peel and seed the cantaloupes. Cut them into chunks and purée in a blender or food processor. Add sweetener, if desired, and mix until completely dissolved. Add the ice cubes, stir and chill for about 30 minutes before serving; add more water if too thick. Serves 4-6.

CASHEW MILK (also see NUT MILK p. 23)

2 cups cashew pieces
3 cups water

Process the cashew pieces in a food processor or blender to a fine meal. Add the water and blend again. Good in all milk-based sauces, over hot cereals and in puddings and custards. Makes 1 quart.

FIG LASSI

2/3 cup buttermilk
1/3 cup syrup from soaked dried figs (see FIGS WITH
   CREAM p. 76)
Ice chips

Combine the buttermilk with the fig syrup and stir.
Add ice chips and garnish with a sprig of fresh mint.
Serves 1.

FIZZY FRUIT PUNCH

Use natural, unsweetened juices:
Apple juice
Pineapple juice
Grape juice
Guava juice
Seltzer water
Ice chips or cubes

TO SERVE 1:
Mix all or any combination of the juices to fill half a
glass; add the seltzer water and ice and serve with
sprig of fresh mint.

TO SERVE 4:
Fill a quart pitcher half full with all or any combination of the juices. Add the seltzer water and ice to
fill the pitcher and serve with fresh mint in each
glass.

FRESH FRUIT SMOOTHIES

In a blender or food processor, place the suggested fruit combinations (or experiment with your own); add 1 Tbsp. unsweetened protein powder, if desired, and blend until smooth. Add crushed ice or seltzer water, and serve. Each combination makes about 1 cup.

1. 1/2 banana, frozen
   3 strawberries, frozen
   1/2 cup apple juice

2. 1/2 cup skim milk or NUT MILK p. 23
   2 tsp. plain yogurt
   1/2 tsp. vanilla extract
   1/2 papaya, banana, peach, mango or a similar fleshy fruit
   Cinnamon to taste

3. 1 cup unsweetened pineapple juice, chilled
   1/2 banana, frozen

4. 1 cup fresh pineapple chunks
   1/2 cup strawberries

5. 1 cup seedless grapes
   1/4 cup blueberries
   1/2 tsp. vanilla extract

6. 1/2 cup fresh orange juice
   1/4 cup fresh grapefruit juice
   1/2 cup fresh pineapple chunks
   A sprinkle of freshly grated coconut

7. 1 cup cherries, pitted
   1 peach, pitted
   1 nectarine, pitted

8. 1/2 cup apple juice
   4 apricots
   4 plums
   1/2 cup pitted cherries
   1/2 banana

9. 2 Tbsp. lemon juice
   2 Tbsp. lime juice
   1/4 cup tangerine juice
   1/2 cup orange juice concentrate
   1/2 tsp. vanilla extract

10. 1/3 cup apple juice
    1/3 cup apricot nectar
    3 fresh apricots or 6 presoaked, dried apricots
    1/2 apple
    1/2 tsp. vanilla extract

11. 1 cup coconut milk or NUT MILK p. 23
    1/4 cup raspberries
    2 Tbsp. plain yogurt, optional
    1/2 tsp. vanilla extract

12. 1 cup orange juice
    1 Tbsp. natural cranberry concentrate
    1 tsp. lemon juice
    Sprinkle of cinnamon

13. 1/2 ripe banana
    1/2 tsp. PEANUT BUTTER p. 10
    1 Tbsp. carob powder
    1 cup low-fat milk or NUT MILK p. 23

14. 1/2 cup apple juice
    1/2 cup unsweetened prune juice
    1 tsp. CASHEW BUTTER p. 2
    1 tsp. plain yogurt, optional

15. 1 cup fresh pineapple chunks
    1 Tbsp. natural, unsweetened black cherry
        concentrate
    1/4 cup orange juice

16. 1/2 cup apple juice
    1/2 cup raspberries
    1 Tbsp. fresh lime juice

17. 1 cup coconut milk
    1 medium peach
    2 Tbsp. plain yogurt
    1/2 tsp. vanilla extract

18. 1/4 cup chamomile tea (1 tsp. loose chamomile or
        1 tea bag steeped in 1 cup boiling water)
    1/2 Tbsp. plain yogurt
    2 Tbsp. unsweetened pineapple juice

19. 1/4 cup peppermint tea (1 tsp. fresh peppermint
        leaves or 1 tea bag steeped in 1 cup boiling
        water)
    1 cup apple juice
    1 Tbsp. fresh lemon juice

20. 1/4 cup fennel tea (1 Tbsp. crushed fennel seeds
        steeped in 1 cup boiling water)
    1/4 cup fresh orange juice
    1/2 cup raspberries or strawberries
    1/4 cup sparkling water

FRUIT SODA

1 Tbsp. unsweetened frozen or bottled fruit juice
    concentrate (apple, apricot, black cherry,
    cranberry, grape, orange, pineapple, strawberry,
    etc., or a combination)
1 cup sparkling water (naturally carbonated)
Crushed ice

Place the concentrate in a tall glass; stir in the sparkling water. Add the crushed ice and serve with a slice of fresh fruit. Serves 1.

MYSTERY MILK

3 1/2 cups NUT MILK p. 23
1/4 cup ground sesame seeds
Sweetener to taste (maple syrup, rice syrup or apple
    juice concentrate)
1 tsp. vanilla extract
Pinch of sea salt

Combine all the ingredients in a food processor or blender and process until smooth. Makes 1 quart.

VARIATIONS:
1. Add any or all of the following to the above recipe:
    1/2 banana
    3 Tbsp. carob powder (more to taste)
    1/2 cup ground sunflower seeds
2. Add more sweetener and freeze in popsicle molds.

NUT MILK

1 cup nuts (blanched almonds, cashews, pecans, etc.)
3 cups water
2 tsp. sweetener (barley malt, carob, rice syrup, maple
    syrup, apple juice concentrate)
1 tsp. vanilla extract

Grind the nuts in a blender or food processor until finely powdered; add the water and blend for 3 minutes. Strain, if desired, and reserve the nut pulp for cereal or baking. Then add the sweetener and vanilla; mix well. Serve hot or cold. Makes 1 quart.

For these recipes, a juicer rather than a blender or food processor makes a great difference in the taste and texture of the juices. Wash any of the suggested vegetable combinations (or experiment with your own combinations) and process in the juicer. Adjust the seasoning and enjoy. Try adding different kinds of sprouts for variety. Each combination makes about 1 cup.

1. 1/2 medium cucumber
   1 organic carrot
   2 stalks celery
   Lemon juice
   Sea salt to taste

2. 1 tomato
   1 slice green pepper
   1/2 cucumber
   1 stalk celery
   1 green onion
   1/2 cup alfalfa sprouts

3. 2 tomatoes
   3 stalks celery
   Sea salt and ground pepper to taste

4. 2 large organic carrots
   2 stalks celery

5. 2 large organic carrots
   1/2 cucumber

6. 1 cucumber
   12-15 fresh green beans
   3 radishes
   Lemon juice
   Sea salt to taste

7. 1 large tomato
   1/2 cup watercress
   Lemon juice
   Sea salt to taste

8. 1 large tomato
   2 stalks celery
   1/2 large organic carrot
   Small bunch watercress
   1 large sprig parsley
   Squeeze fresh lemon

9. 2 tomatoes
   1 large sprig parsley
   1 green onion
   1 small stalk celery
   Sea salt and freshly ground
   pepper to taste

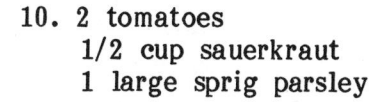

10. 2 tomatoes
    1/2 cup sauerkraut
    1 large sprig parsley

SPICED APPLE CIDER

1 quart apple juice
2 cinnamon sticks
6 whole cloves
2 slices fresh lemon or orange

Combine all the ingredients in a large saucepan and simmer to blend flavors. Serve when thoroughly warmed. Makes 4 cups.

SWEET LASSI

1 pint plain yogurt
2 cups ice water
1/4 cup sweetener (maple or rice syrup, apple juice concentrate, etc.)
Pinch of nutmeg
Dash of rosewater

Beat the yogurt and water together. Add the sweetener, nutmeg and rosewater; blend again and serve with ice slivers in a chilled glass. For variety, blend in frozen fruit such as strawberries. Makes 1 quart.

Breads

Apple Muffins, 28
Apricot-Corn Bread, 28
Banana-Nut Biscuits, 29
Banana-Nut Bread, 30
Buttermilk Biscuits, 30
Cinnamon Buns, 31
Corn Muffins, 32
Cranberry-Nut Bread, 32
Fruit and Nut Turnovers, 33
Hush Puppies, 34
Millet Muffins, 34
Orange-Soy Muffins, 35
Pumpkin Bread, 36
Raisin-Nut Bread, 36
Rice-Soy Bread, 37
Whole Wheat-Apricot Bread, 38
Whole Wheat Bread, 39
Whole Wheat Crepes, 40
Whole Wheat Crescent Rolls, 41
Whole Wheat Pita Bread, 42

APPLE MUFFINS

1 1/4 cups flour (whole wheat, soy, rice, etc.)
2 tsp. low-sodium baking powder
1/4 tsp. each baking soda and sea salt
2 Tbsp. oil
1/2 cup apple juice concentrate
2 Tbsp. maple or rice syrup
1 egg or equivalent egg replacer
1/2 cup plain yogurt
1 cup chopped apples

Preheat the oven to 350°F. Sift the dry ingredients together in a large bowl. Combine the wet ingredients and stir into the flour mixture. Fold in the apples and pour into buttered muffin tins. Bake for 25-30 minutes, until golden brown. Serve hot with APPLE SAUCE p. 180. Makes 10 muffins.

APRICOT-CORN BREAD

3/4 cup dried apricots
2 cups cornmeal
1/4 tsp. sea salt
1 Tbsp. low-sodium baking powder
1 tsp. baking soda
1/2 cup chopped nuts
1 Tbsp. corn oil
1 cup buttermilk
1 cup plain yogurt
2 eggs or equivalent egg replacer

Continued next page...

Preheat the oven to 350°F. Soak the apricots in hot water for 30 minutes; drain and chop finely. Combine the dry ingredients in a large mixing bowl. Combine the remaining ingredients and stir into the cornmeal mixture; pour into an oiled 8-inch square baking pan. Bake for about 35-40 minutes, until browned; serve hot with butter or DRIED FRUIT JAM p. 183. Serves 4-6.

BANANA-NUT BISCUITS

2 1/2 cups sifted, unbleached flour
1 Tbsp. low-sodium baking powder
1/2 tsp. baking soda
1/4 tsp. sea salt, optional
1/4 tsp. cinnamon
1/3 cup melted butter or soy margarine
1/2 banana
3/4 cup buttermilk
3 Tbsp. apple juice concentrate
1/3 cup finely chopped walnuts
1/3 cup raisins or currants

Preheat the oven to 450°F. Sift the dry ingredients together in a large bowl; cut in the butter with a pastry blender. Mash the banana and mix with the buttermilk, apple juice concentrate, walnuts, and raisins. Stir the buttermilk mixture into the dry ingredients until it forms a ball of dough; roll out on a floured pastry sheet about 1/2-inch thick and cut with a biscuit cutter or large drinking glass. Place the biscuits on an oiled or non-stick baking sheet and brush the tops lightly with buttermilk. Bake for 10-15 minutes, until golden brown. Serve hot with BANANA SAUCE p. 181. Makes 2 dozen.

BANANA-NUT BREAD

4 cups flour (try 2 cups whole wheat, 2 cups unbleached or 1 cup rice flour, 3 cups soy flour)
1 Tbsp. low-sodium baking powder
1 tsp. baking soda
1/2-1 tsp. sea salt
1 cup melted butter or soy margarine
1/2 cup apple juice concentrate
1/4 cup maple syrup
2 eggs or equivalent egg replacer
5-6 overripe bananas, mashed
1/2 cup buttermilk
1 cup chopped walnuts
1/2 cup raisins or currants

Preheat the oven to 350°F. Sift the dry ingredients together; cut in the butter with a pastry blender. Combine the remaining ingredients; stir into the dry mix. Turn into 2 oiled loaf pans and bake for 45-50 minutes or until a toothpick comes out clean. Cool in the pans for 10 minutes, then turn onto a rack. Serve with butter and/or BANANA SAUCE p. 181. Makes 2 loaves.

BUTTERMILK BISCUITS

2 cups unbleached flour
1 Tbsp. low-sodium baking powder
1/4 tsp. baking soda
1/4 tsp. sea salt, optional
1/3 cup melted butter or soy margarine
3/4 cup buttermilk

Continued next page...

Preheat the oven to 450°F. Sift the dry ingredients together in a large bowl; cut in the butter with a fork or pastry blender. Stir in the buttermilk until it forms a dough ball and gently knead about 10 times. Roll the dough out on a floured pastry sheet to a 1/2-inch thickness and cut with a biscuit cutter or large drinking glass. Place the biscuits on an oiled or non-stick baking sheet and brush the tops lightly with buttermilk. Bake for 10-15 minutes, until the biscuits are golden brown. Makes about 1 dozen.

CINNAMON BUNS

1 cup hot NUT MILK p. 23, soy milk or water
1 Tbsp. active dry yeast
1/4 cup maple syrup
3 Tbsp. oil
3 cups flour (half unbleached, half whole wheat or 1 cup rice flour, 2 cups soy flour)
1 tsp. cinnamon
1 tsp. sea salt
1/2 cup raisins
1 cup chopped nuts

Preheat the oven to 350°F. Combine the wet ingredients and the yeast; set aside for 5 minutes. Sift the flour, cinnamon and salt together and stir into the yeast mixture. Knead until smooth; cover and allow to rise. Add the raisins and nuts and squeeze into the dough with your fingers until evenly mixed. Pinch off dough and roll into 1-inch balls. Place 3 balls into each oiled cup of a muffin tin. Allow to rise in a warm place until doubled in size. Bake for about 30 minutes or until browned. Makes about 2 dozen buns.

CORN MUFFINS

3 cups cornmeal
1 Tbsp. low-sodium baking powder
1 tsp. baking soda
1/4 tsp. sea salt
1/4 cup melted butter or soy margarine
1 cup buttermilk
3 Tbsp. apple juice concentrate
1 cup hot water

Preheat the oven to 400°F. Combine the dry ingredients and mix well; cut in the butter. Stir in the buttermilk and apple juice concentrate; add the hot water to make a soupy batter. Pour into oiled tins (3/4 full) and bake for 15-20 minutes. (For a spicy change, add 1/4 tsp. cayenne pepper and 1 cup cooked corn kernels to the batter.) Makes 1 1/2 dozen.

CRANBERRY-NUT BREAD

2 cups flour (1 cup each unbleached and whole wheat
    or 3/4 cup rice flour and 1 1/4 cups soy flour)
1 Tbsp. low-sodium baking powder
1/2-1 tsp. sea salt
1/4 cup oil
1 tsp. grated orange peel
1/2 cup sweetener (maple syrup, rice syrup, etc.)
1/3 cup orange juice
1 egg or equivalent egg replacer
1 cup coarsely chopped fresh cranberries
1/2 cup chopped nuts

Continued next page...

Preheat the oven to 350°F. Sift the dry ingredients together. Combine the oil, peel, sweetener, juice and egg or replacer; add to the dry ingredients, mixing just enough to moisten. Fold in the berries and nuts and turn into an oiled 9-inch loaf pan; bake for 1 hour. Cool and slice to serve. Makes 1 loaf.

FRUIT AND NUT TURNOVERS

2 cups diced apples and 3/4 cup APPLE SAUCE p. 180
    blueberries and BLUEBERRY SAUCE p. 181 or
    pitted cherries and CHERRY SAUCE p. 182 or
    raisins and RAISIN SAUCE p. 184 or
    strawberries and STRAWBERRY SAUCE p. 186
1/2 cup chopped nuts
BUTTERMILK BISCUIT p. 30 dough

Preheat the oven to 400°F. Combine the fruit and its corresponding sauce in a small saucepan; simmer until the fruit is tender. Add the nuts and set aside. On a floured pastry sheet, roll out the biscuit dough into a large rectangle; cut into twelve 4-inch squares. Place the squares on buttered baking sheets and spoon about 1 tablespoon of the fruit and nut mixture into the center of each square. Fold over the opposite corners, forming a triangle. Press the edges together with a fork and prick the tops. Bake for 15-20 minutes and serve, topped with any leftover filling. Makes 1 dozen.

HUSH PUPPIES

2 cups cornmeal
1 Tbsp. flour (unbleached, whole wheat, soy, rice, etc.)
1/2 tsp. baking soda
1/2-1 tsp. sea salt
1 egg or equivalent egg replacer
3 Tbsp. minced onion
1 cup buttermilk

Preheat a deep-fryer to 350-375°F. Combine the dry ingredients in a mixing bowl. Combine the beaten egg or replacer with the onion and buttermilk; stir into the cornmeal mixture. Drop by the teaspoonful into the hot oil; remove when golden brown and drain on paper towels. Serve with BLACK-EYED PEA SALAD p. 151, or STEWED OKRA p. 227. Makes 2 dozen.

MILLET MUFFINS

2 1/2 cups millet flour (grind raw millet into a powder)
1 cup brown rice flour
1 Tbsp. low-sodium baking powder
1/2 tsp. baking soda
1/4-1/2 tsp. sea salt, optional
2 Tbsp. melted butter or soy margarine
1 cup buttermilk
2 Tbsp. sweetener (apple juice concentrate or maple or rice syrup)
1 cup hot water

Continued next page...

Preheat the oven to 400°F. Sift together the dry ingredients; cut in the butter with a pastry blender. Combine the buttermilk and sweetener and stir into the dry mixture. Slowly add the hot water until the mixture is fluffy but a little soupy. Pour into oiled muffin tins (3/4 full) and bake for 15 minutes. Makes 1 1/2 dozen.

VARIATION:
Add 2 Tbsp. more sweetener, 1 tsp. vanilla extract, 1/2 tsp. cinnamon and 1/2 cup shredded coconut to the batter and bake as directed.

ORANGE-SOY MUFFINS

1 1/2 cups soy flour
1 cup rice flour
1 Tbsp. low-sodium baking powder
2 eggs or equivalent egg replacer
1/4 cup sweetener (orange juice concentrate or maple
　　or rice syrup)
1 tsp. grated orange peel
1 Tbsp. oil or butter
1 1/4 cups milk or NUT MILK p. 23
1/4 cup chopped walnuts
1/4 cup raisins

Preheat the oven to 350°F. Sift the dry ingredients together in a large mixing bowl. Combine the remaining ingredients and stir into the flour mixture. Pour into oiled muffin tins and bake for 20-25 minutes. Makes 1 dozen.

PUMPKIN BREAD

1 1/2 cups puréed cooked pumpkin
1/2 cup melted butter or soy margarine
1 tsp. vanilla extract
1/2 cup maple syrup
1/8 tsp. grated lemon peel
1 Tbsp. low-sodium baking powder
1 tsp. sea salt
1 tsp. cinnamon
1/4 tsp. allspice
1 3/4 cups pastry flour (unbleached, whole wheat, soy)
1 cup chopped nuts, optional

Preheat the oven to 350°F. Combine all the wet ingredients; mix well. Sift the dry ingredients together and slowly beat into the pumpkin mixture. Pour into a large, oiled loaf pan and bake for about 50-55 minutes. Cool and slice. Makes 1 loaf.

RAISIN-NUT BREAD

2 1/2 cups flour (whole wheat or soy-rice combination)
1/2-1 tsp. sea salt
1 Tbsp. low-sodium baking powder
1/2 tsp. baking soda
1/2 tsp. cinnamon
1/2 cup molasses or maple syrup
1/4 cup oil or melted butter or soy margarine
1 1/2 cups buttermilk
1/2 cup each raisins and chopped walnuts
1 Tbsp. grated orange peel

Continued next page...

Sift together the dry ingredients. Combine the remaining ingredients, and stir into the flour mixture. Pour into a buttered loaf pan; let the mixture stand for 20 minutes. Preheat the oven to 375°F. and bake for 45 minutes-1 hour. Makes 1 loaf.

RICE-SOY BREAD

2 Tbsp. sweetener (molasses, maple or rice syrup, etc.)
2 cups warm water
1 packet active dry yeast
2 cups brown rice flour
1 cup soy flour
2 Tbsp. oil
1/2 tsp. sea salt, optional

Allow the refrigerated ingredients to warm to room temperature. Combine the sweetener and warm water in a large bowl; add the yeast and set aside for 5 minutes. Stir in the remaining ingredients to form a thick batter. Pour into 2 loaf pans; cover and set aside at room temperature (<u>not</u> a warm place) until the dough almost rises to the top of the pans. Preheat the oven to 400°F. and bake for 30-35 minutes. Turn onto a wire rack to cool. Slice and serve with butter. Makes 2 loaves.

WHOLE WHEAT-APRICOT BREAD

1/2 cup water
1/4 cup maple syrup
1/2 cup chopped dried apricots
1/2 cup raisins
1 1/2 cups whole wheat flour
2 tsp. low-sodium baking powder
1/2 tsp. baking soda
1/2 tsp. sea salt
2 eggs or equivalent egg replacer
1/4 cup melted butter or soy margarine
1 tsp. vanilla extract
1/2 cup chopped walnuts

Preheat the oven to 350°F. In a medium saucepan, combine the water, maple syrup, apricots and raisins. Bring to a boil; remove from the heat and cool. In a large mixing bowl, sift together the dry ingredients; stir in the apricot mixture and the remaining ingredients and turn into an oiled 9-inch loaf pan. Bake for 40-45 minutes. Cool and serve. Makes 1 large loaf.

WHOLE WHEAT BREAD

3 cups warm water
3/4 cup sweetener (maple syrup, molasses, rice syrup or barley malt)
2-3 packets active dry yeast
1/4 cup oil or melted butter
5 cups unsifted whole wheat flour
3 tsp. sea salt
2 additional cups whole wheat flour
Extra flour for kneading

Allow the refrigerated ingredients to warm to room temperature. Combine the warm water, sweetener and active dry yeast in a large mixing bowl; set aside for at least 5 minutes. Add the oil, 5 cups flour and salt. Beat in <u>very</u> well (100 strokes by hand) or the bread will be heavy. Add the 2 additional cups of flour or enough to make a stiff dough.

Turn the dough onto a heavily floured bread board or pastry sheet, and knead until smooth and elastic. Lightly coat the dough ball with a little oil; place in an oiled bowl, cover and set aside to rise in a warm place for about 1 hour or until doubled in size.

Punch the dough to the original size; cover and let rise again until doubled. Knead to the original size and divide into 3 equal parts; shape into 3 loaves and place in buttered 1-lb. loaf pans. Cover the loaves and allow to rise until the dough reaches the top of the pans. Preheat the oven to 350°F. Bake for 50 minutes or until well browned. Brush the crust with butter and turn onto a wire rack to cool. Makes 3 loaves.

WHOLE WHEAT CREPES

2 eggs or equivalent egg replacer
1/2 tsp. sea salt
1 cup whole wheat flour
1 1/4 cups milk or NUT MILK p. 23
Oil for frying

Beat the eggs or egg replacer and salt together; stir in the flour. Add the milk and beat to a thin, smooth batter (add extra milk if necessary). Set aside for about 20 minutes.

Meanwhile, heat a crepe pan or a 7-inch, heavy-bottomed skillet on medium heat. When hot, brush it with oil and pour in 2 Tbsp. of the batter. Tilt the pan quickly so that the batter spreads evenly over the bottom of the skillet. When the batter is set and the surface has turned dull, turn it over gently and cook the other side. Remove the crepe from the pan; place it on a lightly buttered plate on top of a pan of boiling water (to keep it warm and moist while cooking the rest). Repeat the process for each crepe, stacking the crepes on top of each other, until all the batter is used.

Fill the crepes with vegetables or fruit and an accompanying sauce; serve immediately. (The cooked crepes may be refrigerated or individually wrapped and frozen to fill and serve later.) Serves 4.

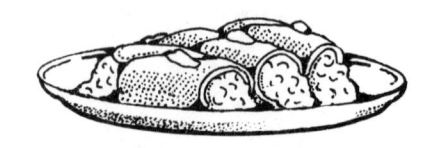

WHOLE WHEAT CRESCENT ROLLS

WHOLE WHEAT BREAD dough p. 39
Butter
Sesame or poppy seeds

Follow the directions for the WHOLE WHEAT BREAD up to the division of the dough into loaves. Divide the bread into 4 equal sections and roll them into balls. One at a time, turn the dough balls onto a floured pastry sheet and roll the dough out to 1/8-inch thickness. Coat the surface with butter and sesame or poppy seeds.

Cut the dough into 3-inch squares with a knife; then cut each square in half diagonally to form triangles. Roll each triangle, starting with the wide side, and gently stretch horizontally while rolling.

Bend the rolls into a crescent shape and place on a buttered baking sheet; let rise about 10 minutes. Preheat the oven to 350°F. and bake for about 10-15 minutes, until browned. Makes 2-3 dozen.

WHOLE WHEAT PITA BREAD

1 pkg. active dry yeast
2 cups lukewarm water
1 cup unbleached flour
1 1/2 tsp. sea salt
3 3/4-4 cups whole wheat flour
Extra water as needed

In a large mixing bowl, dissolve the yeast in the warm water and set aside for 10 minutes. Stir in the unbleached flour and salt. Gradually work in the whole wheat flour, using a little extra water as needed to make a workable but not soft dough. Knead until elastic (about 10 minutes); cover with a damp cloth and set aside to rise at room temperature for several hours. When the dough is doubled in size, deflate the air bubbles and divide into 12 equal portions.

Preheat the oven to 450°F. Roll each portion on a lightly floured board to form an 8-inch circle about 1/8-inch thick. Set aside to rise on unoiled baking sheets until almost doubled in size, about 15 minutes. Flip the breads over several times while rising. Bake 4 pitas at a time in mid oven for about 5 minutes, until puffed up and lightly browned. Cool thoroughly and store in plastic bags.

Breakfasts

Basic Granola, 44
Blueberry-Oatmeal Waffles, 45
Buckwheat Waffles, 46
Cinnamon Oatmeal with Bananas, 46
Cornmeal Waffles, 47
Date Rice, 47
Ginger-Nut Waffles, 48
Granola-Fruit Yogurt, 48
Hardy Grain Pancakes, 49
Hoe Cakes, 49
Homemade Cream of Rice Cereal, 50
Kasha-Rice Cereal, 50
Millet-Sesame Cereal, 51
Scrambled Tofu I, 52
Scrambled Tofu II, 52
Spicy Fruit Pancakes, 53
Toasted Oatmeal, 54
Wheatberry Cereal, 54
Whole-Grain Pancakes, 55

BASIC GRANOLA

BASIC RECIPE:
1/4 cup oil
1/4 cup maple syrup
1/2 tsp. vanilla extract
3 cups oatmeal
1/4 tsp. sea salt
1/2 cup chopped nuts
1/2 cup raisins or chopped dried fruit

DRY INGREDIENTS:
Rolled or flaked oats, wheat, rye, soy, rice, corn, etc.; assorted seeds; wheat germ and assorted brans; unsweetened protein powder and powdered milk; salt, cinnamon, ginger, lemon peel and other spices; chopped or sliced almonds, cashews, pecans, walnuts or other nuts.

WET INGREDIENTS:
Oil; melted butter or soy margarine; maple syrup; fruit juice concentrates; molasses; rice syrup; barley malt; vanilla extract.

FRUIT:
Shredded coconut; raisins; chopped dried dates, apples, figs, apricots, pineapple, prunes, etc.

Use the BASIC RECIPE and add any of the alternative dry and wet ingredients, keeping a ratio of 6 cups dry ingredients to 1 cup wet ingredients and 1 cup fruit and nuts. Combine the wet ingredients in one bowl and the dry in another; mix each well. Then combine, mix and roast in a shallow pan at 250°F. for 30 minutes. After roasting, add the dried fruit and nuts. The basic recipe makes 4 cups.

BLUEBERRY-OATMEAL WAFFLES

1 cup fresh or frozen blueberries
1/2-1 cup chopped pecans
4 cups oatmeal
1/4 cup rice flour or cornmeal
1 tsp. sea salt
1 tsp. ginger
1 tsp. cinnamon
4 cups milk, NUT MILK p. 23 or water
1/4 cup oil
1 Tbsp. lemon juice
2 tsp. vanilla extract
1/4 cup sweetener (maple syrup, fruit juice concentrate, etc.)

Set the blueberries and nuts aside. Mix the dry ingredients in a large bowl; stir in the milk. Combine the remaining ingredients and stir into the oatmeal mixture; refrigerate until thick, or prepare and refrigerate the night before. When ready to cook, fold in the blueberries and pecans; spoon the batter onto a preheated waffle iron and cook for 7-10 minutes. Serve with BLUEBERRY SAUCE p. 181, maple syrup or plain yogurt. Makes 8 waffles.

VARIATIONS:
1. Omit the blueberries and substitute other finely chopped fresh fruit.
2. Omit the blueberries; cook, top with fresh fruit and whipped cream and serve as a dessert.
3. In place of the 4 cups oats, use 2 cups oats and 2 cups cooked rice; also reduce the milk to 3 cups instead of 4.

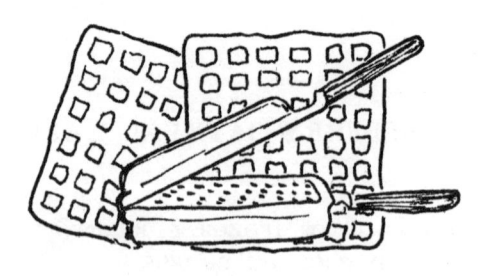

BUCKWHEAT WAFFLES

1 1/2 cups buckwheat flour
1/2 cup powdered milk or 1/4 cup finely ground nutmeat
1/2 tsp. sea salt
3 tsp. low-sodium baking powder
2 cups milk or NUT MILK p. 23
2 Tbsp. sweetener (maple syrup, molasses, apple juice
   concentrate)
1/4 cup oil
2 eggs or equivalent egg replacer
Water to thin

Mix the dry ingredients together in a large mixing bowl. Combine the wet ingredients and stir into the flour mixture. Add water to thin, if necessary; pour onto a preheated waffle iron. Makes 8 waffles.

CINNAMON OATMEAL WITH BANANAS

Prepare the oatmeal as directed for the quantity desired. (Or make in a thermos bottle: see HARDY GRAIN PANCAKES p. 49.) When the oatmeal is cooked, stir in 1/8 tsp. cinnamon per serving and top with sliced bananas and 1 tsp. chopped nuts. Add a little fruit juice concentrate or maple syrup for sweetener and NUT MILK p. 23, if desired.

CORNMEAL WAFFLES

1 1/2 cups cornmeal
1/2 cup powdered milk or 1/4 cup finely ground nutmeat
1/2 tsp. sea salt
3 tsp. low-sodium baking powder
1 tsp. baking soda
2 cups buttermilk or yogurt
2 Tbsp. sweetener (maple syrup, molasses, or apple juice concentrate)
1/4 cup oil
2 eggs or equivalent egg replacer
Water to thin

Mix the dry ingredients together in a large mixing bowl. Combine the wet ingredients and add to the dry mixture. Stir gently; add water to thin, if necessary. Pour onto a preheated waffle iron. Makes 8 waffles.

DATE RICE

1 cup BROWN RICE p. 132, cooked
1/4 cup finely chopped dates
CASHEW MILK p. 17 or CREAM p. 182

This is a good way to use leftover brown rice. Combine the cooked rice, dates and CASHEW MILK or CREAM and serve cold or heat gently, but <u>do not boil</u>. Serves 1.

GINGER-NUT WAFFLES

1 1/4 cups flour (whole wheat or rice-soy combination)
1/2 cup powdered milk or 1/4 cup finely ground nutmeat
1/2 tsp. sea salt
3 tsp. low-sodium baking powder
1 tsp. baking soda
1 tsp. cinnamon
3 tsp. ground ginger
1 1/2 cups buttermilk or yogurt
1/4 cup sweetener (maple syrup, molasses or fruit juice concentrate)
1/4 cup oil
3 eggs or equivalent egg replacer
1 tsp. vanilla extract
3/4 cup water to thin
1 cup chopped nuts (pecans, walnuts, cashews)

Mix the dry ingredients together in a large mixing bowl. Combine the wet ingredients and add to the flour mixture. Gently stir in the chopped nuts and pour onto a preheated waffle iron. Makes 8 waffles.

GRANOLA-FRUIT YOGURT

1/2 cup BASIC GRANOLA p. 44
1/2 cup sliced bananas, peaches, berries, etc. (any favorite fruit or combination, in season)
1 cup plain yogurt

Use the BASIC GRANOLA recipe or a health food store brand and serve with the fruit over yogurt. Serves 1.

HARDY GRAIN PANCAKES

2 cups oatmeal, cooked
3 cups BROWN RICE p. 132, cooked

TO COOK THE OATMEAL:
Place 1 1/4 cups uncooked oatmeal in a wide-mouth, 1-quart thermos bottle. Pour in enough boiling water to fill and stir. Close the thermos and lay it on its side. In the morning the oatmeal will be thick and sticky and ready to use for pancakes.

TO MAKE THE PANCAKES:
Mix the oatmeal and rice together well, forming a sticky ball; divide into 4 parts. Press each part into the bottom of a non-stick skillet to form a large, 1/2-inch thick pancake. Cook on medium-high heat, until both sides are crisp (about 30 minutes); flip often to keep from burning. Serve with butter and syrup or a fruit sauce. Makes 4 large pancakes.

HOE CAKES

2 cups cornmeal
1 tsp. sea salt
HOT water

Mix the cornmeal and salt in a mixing bowl; moisten with very hot water and set aside for 1 hour. Shape into 1/2-inch thick, flat cakes with your hands and fry in a little oil on a hot skillet or griddle until golden brown on both sides. Serve with butter and maple syrup or a fruit sauce. Makes 6 pancakes.

HOMEMADE CREAM OF RICE CEREAL

1/4 cup homemade cream of rice (instructions below)
1 1/2 cups water
1/4 tsp. sea salt, optional
2 Tbsp. currants
1/3 cup BROWN RICE p. 132, cooked

TO PREPARE THE CREAM OF RICE:
Place 2 cups of uncooked brown rice in a heavy skillet; heat on medium until lightly toasted, stirring constantly. Cool and place in a Vita-Mix® or grain grinder and chop to a fine powder. Store in a covered jar and use for cereal or to thicken soups and sauces.

TO COOK THE CEREAL:
Bring the water and salt to a boil; slowly add 3 Tbsp. of the cream of rice and stir with a whisk. Lower the heat and simmer for about 15 minutes, stirring frequently. Add the currants and brown rice, stir and serve. A sweetener and/or NUT MILK p. 23 can be added, if desired. Serves 1.

KASHA-RICE CEREAL

1 1/2 cups water
1/4 cup whole or coarse kasha (roasted buckwheat)
1/2 cup uncooked brown rice
1/8 tsp. sea salt, optional
1/4 cup raisins
1/4 cup chopped dates
NUT MILK p. 23 to taste

Continued next page...

Bring the water to a boil. Add the kasha, brown rice, and salt; cover and simmer for 1 hour, until the water is absorbed. Mix in the raisins, dates and NUT MILK and serve. Serves 2.

(Cook double or triple the grain recipe. Later, reheat the leftovers in a non-stick skillet, before adding the raisins, dates and milk.)

MILLET-SESAME CEREAL

1 1/2 cups water
1/3 cup toasted millet-sesame mix (instructions below)
1/8 tsp. sea salt
1/4 cup sliced fresh fruit in season
CASHEW MILK p. 17 or ALMOND MILK p. 16

TO PREPARE THE MILLET-SESAME MIX:
Place 1 cup raw millet and 1/4 cup ground raw sesame seeds in a heavy skillet; stir over medium heat until lightly toasted. Cool and store in a covered jar; cook as needed for breakfast cereal, as a vegetable stuffing or as a grain side dish.

TO COOK THE CEREAL:
In a saucepan, bring the water, millet-sesame mix and salt to a boil. Cover and simmer until the water has cooked down and the millet is light and fluffy, about 20 minutes. Add the sliced fruit and CASHEW or ALMOND MILK and serve. For additional sweetener, the fruit can be marinated in fruit juice concentrate and added along with the milk. Serves 1.

SCRAMBLED TOFU I

2 Tbsp. oil
1/4 cup chopped green onions with tops
1 lb. tofu, crumbled
1/4 cup cooked carrots, minced
1/8 tsp. garlic powder
1/2 tsp. dried or Dijon-style mustard
Sea salt and pepper to taste

In a large skillet, sauté the green onions in the oil. Add the remaining ingredients and mix well. Sauté until well heated. Garnish with fresh parsley and serve like scrambled eggs, with whole-grain toast or rice. Serves 2.

SCRAMBLED TOFU II

2 Tbsp. oil
1/4 cup chopped green onions with tops
1/4 cup chopped celery
1 lb. tofu, crumbled
1 tsp. curry powder
1/2 tsp. tumeric powder
Cayenne pepper to taste
Garlic powder to taste
Sea salt and pepper to taste

In a large skillet, sauté the green onions and celery in the oil. Add the remaining ingredients and mix well. Sauté until well heated. Garnish with fresh parsley and serve like scrambled eggs, with whole-grain toast or rice. Serves 2.

SPICY FRUIT PANCAKES

1 1/4 cups whole wheat flour
2 1/2 tsp. low-sodium baking powder
1/2 tsp. cinnamon
1/2 tsp. nutmeg
1/2 tsp. ground coriander
1/4 tsp. sea salt
1/4 cup powdered milk or finely ground nutmeat
2 eggs or equivalent egg replacer
2 Tbsp. oil
2 Tbsp. maple syrup
1 cup water
Any one of the following fruits:
    1/2 cup fresh berries
    1 peeled apple, grated
    1 large banana, mashed
    1/2 cup raisins
    1-2 peaches, chopped
    1 small mango, chopped
    1/2 cup chopped, pitted dates
    1/2 cup chopped figs

In a large bowl, combine the flour, baking powder, spices, salt and powdered milk or nutmeat; mix well. In a small mixing bowl, combine the egg replacer, oil, maple syrup and water; mix well and stir into the dry mixture. Gently fold in the fruit and pour 1/4 cup of the batter for each pancake into a preheated, oiled skillet. Turn the pancakes when bubbles appear on the top and the underside is lightly browned. Continue to cook until both sides are browned. Serve with butter; syrup is usually not needed. Makes 10-12 pancakes.

TOASTED OATMEAL

1/4 cup toasted oatmeal (instructions below)
1 1/2 cups boiling water
1/4 tsp. sea salt, optional
CASHEW MILK P. 17

TO PREPARE THE TOASTED OATMEAL:
Heat 1 Tbsp. oil in a large skillet; toast 2 cups oatmeal on medium heat, until lightly browned. Cool and store in a covered jar to use as needed for cereal.

TO COOK THE CEREAL:
Bring the water and salt to a boil. Add the oatmeal, simmer for 20 minutes. Serve with CASHEW MILK, cinnamon, raisins, dried fruit or seeds. Serves 1.

WHEATBERRY CEREAL

1 cup wheatberries
2 cups water
1/4 cup raisins
Sweetener to taste (rice or maple syrup, barley malt, molasses, fruit juice concentrate)
1 Tbsp. chopped walnuts
1 tsp. sunflower seeds
Sliced fruit, berries or chopped dried fruit

Place the wheatberries, water and raisins in a crockpot and cook overnight on low heat or cook in a pressure cooker for 40 minutes. When the berries are tender, drain the liquid, stir in the remaining ingredients and serve with NUT MILK P. 23, if desired. Serves 2.

WHOLE-GRAIN PANCAKES

1 1/3 cups whole-grain flour (rice, buckwheat, millet, rye, corn, etc., or a mixture)
3 tsp. low-sodium baking powder
1/4 tsp. sea salt
1 egg or equivalent egg replacer
1 cup NUT MILK p. 23
1/3 cup fruit juice concentrate
1 Tbsp. oil

Oil and heat a griddle or heavy skillet while mixing the batter. (The skillet is hot enough when water bounces off.) In a large bowl, mix the flour, baking powder and salt; set aside. In another bowl, combine the wet ingredients and stir into the flour mixture to form a lumpy batter. Pour 1/4 cup of the batter onto the griddle for each pancake. Cook on medium heat until tiny bubbles form throughout the pancakes and the edges are slightly dry. Turn and brown on the other side. Serve with maple syrup, a fruit sauce, compote or jam. Makes 8 pancakes.

VARIATION:
Fold 1/2 cup berries or chopped fresh fruit into the batter before cooking.

56

Desserts

CANDIES

Almond Butter Balls, 59
Almond Candy, 59
Black Walnut Balls, 60
Carob-Peanut Butter Fudge, 60
Fruit-Nut Balls, 61
Maple-Cashew Butter Fudge, 61
Peanut Butter-Fruit Balls, 62
Pralines, 62

COOKIES

Almond Cookies, 63
Carob Chip-Oatmeal Cookies, 64
Date-Nut Cookies, 65
Fig Roll Cookies, 66
Nutty Cookies, 66
Oatmeal-Fruit Bars, 67
Peanut Butter Cookies, 68
Raisin-Spice Cookies, 68
Sama's Tea Cookies, 69

Continued next page...

FROZEN DESSERTS

Apple-Cherry Popsicles, 70
Banana Sherbet, 70
Frozen Grapes, Bananas
 and Strawberries, 70
Mango Ice Cream, 71
Papaya with Fruit
 Sherbet, 71
Pineapple-Strawberry
 Sherbet, 72
Strawberry Ice Cream, 72

FRUIT DESSERTS

Apple Upside-Down Cake, 73
Baked Apples, 74
B R's Tropical Fruit
 Compote, 74
Carob-Coated Fresh
 Fruit, 75
Deep-Fried Bananas, 76
Figs with Cream, 76
Fig Whip, 77
Fruit "Gello," 77
Fruit Platter, 78
Georgian Fruit Compote, 78

PIE CRUSTS

Almond Pie Crust, 79
Granola Pie Crust, 79
Nutty Tart Shells, 80
Rice Flour Pie Crust, 80

PIES

Almond-Apricot
 Cheesecake, 81
Apple Cobbler, 82
Blueberry-Coconut Cream
 Pie, 82
Blueberry-Mango Pudding
 or Pie, 83
Carob Creme Pie, 84
Cherry-Tapioca Pudding or
 Pie, 84
Fresh Fruit Pie, 85
Peach Cobbler, 86
Pineapple-Tapioca Pudding
 or Pie, 86
Plush Pecan Pie, 87
Sweet Potato Tarts, 88

CANDIES

ALMOND BUTTER BALLS

1/2 cup walnuts
1/4 cup sesame seeds
1/2 cup ALMOND BUTTER p. 2
1/4 cup tahini
1/4 cup chopped dates
1/4 cup chopped dried apricots
1-2 Tbsp. maple syrup, optional

Coarsely chop the walnuts and sesame seeds. Stir in the remaining ingredients, one at a time, until well mixed. Roll into 1-inch balls, chill and serve. Makes about 18.

ALMOND CANDY

1/3 cup butter or soy margarine
1/4 cup maple syrup
3/4 cup slivered almonds

Butter an 8-inch square pan and set aside. Melt the butter in a heavy frying pan and stir in the maple syrup. Add the almonds and cook over medium heat, stirring continuously until the mixture turns golden brown, about 7 minutes. Spread the mixture in the square pan, working quickly while still very hot. With a sharp, buttered knife, cut into squares immediately, then cool. Chill in the refrigerator and store in a covered container. Makes 16 2-inch squares.

BLACK WALNUT BALLS

1 cup black walnuts
1/4 cup sesame seeds
1/4 cup tahini
1/4 cup maple syrup
1/4 cup PEANUT BUTTER p. 10
1/4 cup chopped dried apples

Finely chop the black walnuts and sesame seeds. Stir in the remaining ingredients, one at a time, until well mixed. Roll into 1-inch balls, chill and serve. Makes about 2 dozen.

CAROB-PEANUT BUTTER FUDGE

1/4 cup butter or soy margarine
1/3 cup maple syrup
6 Tbsp. carob powder
1/3 cup milk or CASHEW MILK p. 17 (more if needed)
1/2-1 cup PEANUT BUTTER p. 10 (if unsalted, add 1/4 tsp. sea salt)
1 tsp. vanilla extract
3 cups oatmeal

In a small saucepan, melt the butter; add the syrup and carob and bring to a boil. Add the milk and mix. Simmer for 5 minutes. Remove from the heat; add the peanut butter and vanilla and mix well. Stir in the oatmeal, 1 cup at a time. Drop by the teaspoonful onto wax paper. Let cool and serve. Makes about 3 dozen balls.

FRUIT-NUT BALLS

1 cup dried currants
1/2 cup figs
1/2 cup pitted dates
1/2 cup walnuts
1/2 cup sunflower seeds
Cinnamon to taste

Combine all the ingredients in a food processor and chop coarsely. Mix thoroughly with your hands, then roll into 1-inch balls and chill until ready to serve. Makes about 2 dozen balls.

MAPLE-CASHEW BUTTER FUDGE

1 cup maple syrup
3/4 cup milk or CASHEW MILK p. 17
1/4 cup light cream or CASHEW CREAM p. 182
2 Tbsp. dry milk powder or finely ground cashews
1/2 tsp. sea salt
2 Tbsp. soft CASHEW BUTTER p. 2

Combine the syrup, milk, cream and salt in a saucepan and cook briskly for 15 minutes. Remove from the heat, add the cashew butter and beat until smooth and creamy. Pour into a buttered 8-inch pan and cool. Cut into squares. Makes 16 squares.

PEANUT BUTTER-FRUIT BALLS

1/2 cup PEANUT BUTTER p. 10
1/2 cup finely ground cashews
1/4 cup tahini
2 Tbsp. maple syrup
1/4 cup raisins
1/4 cup chopped dates
Shredded coconut

Set the coconut aside and combine all the remaining ingredients, adding one at a time, until well blended. Roll into 1-inch balls; then roll in the coconut and chill before serving. Makes about 2 dozen.

PRALINES

1/2 cup maple syrup
1/2 cup buttermilk
1/2 tsp. baking soda
Dash of sea salt
1 tsp. butter or soy margarine
3/4 cup pecan pieces

In a saucepan, mix the maple syrup, buttermilk, soda and salt. Cook over high heat for 5 minutes, then add the butter. Continue to cook, stirring often, until the mixture forms a soft ball when dropped into cold water. Then, remove from the heat and cool for 5 minutes. Beat until creamy; then add the pecans. Immediately drop by the tablespoonful onto buttered wax paper to cool. Makes 1 dozen pralines.

COOKIES

ALMOND COOKIES

2 cups flour (soy, brown rice, unbleached wheat or a mixture)
2 tsp. low-sodium baking powder
1/4 tsp. sea salt
1/2 cup blanched almonds, chopped
1/2 cup butter or soy margarine
1/2 cup maple syrup
1 egg or equivalent egg replacer
1 tsp. almond extract
1 tsp. vanilla extract
30 blanched almonds

Oil 2 cookie sheets and preheat the oven to 350°F. Sift the flour, baking powder and salt together. In a small saucepan, melt the butter; stir in the maple syrup, egg or egg replacer, almond extract and chopped almonds. Add to the dry ingredients, a little at a time, and mix well. Roll into 1-inch balls and place on the oiled cookie sheets. Gently press a blanched almond into the center of each ball. (To blanch the almonds, cover them with boiling water and allow them to stand for about 2 minutes; then drain the water and slip the thin brown skins off between your fingertips.) Bake about 20 minutes, until light golden brown; cool and serve. Makes about 30 cookies.

CAROB CHIP-OATMEAL COOKIES

1/2 cup butter or soy margarine
1/4 cup maple syrup
1 egg or equivalent egg replacer
1/2 tsp. vanilla extract
1 1/4 cups sifted flour (unbleached wheat, chickpea or brown rice)
1 cup oatmeal
1/4 tsp. sea salt
2 tsp. low-sodium baking powder
1/4 cup carob chips
1/2 cup raisins
1/2 cup chopped nuts (pecans or walnuts)

Preheat the oven to 350°F. Melt the butter; add the maple syrup, egg or egg replacer and vanilla and beat until creamy. Sift together the flour, oatmeal, salt, and baking powder; stir into the butter mixture. Then add the carob chips, raisins and nuts. Drop the batter by the tablespoonful onto an oiled cookie sheet, about 1/2-inch apart. Bake for 15 minutes or until golden brown. Makes about 1 1/2 dozen.

DATE-NUT COOKIES

2 cups soy flour
1 cup powdered milk
1/2 tsp. sea salt
1 Tbsp. low-sodium baking powder
1 cup chopped nuts
1 cup chopped dates
3 eggs or equivalent egg replacer
3 Tbsp. butter or soy margarine, melted
3/4 cup orange juice
3 Tbsp. maple syrup

Preheat oven to 350°F. In a large bowl, sift together the flour, powdered milk, salt and baking powder. Add the nuts and dates, coating them with the dry mixture. In a separate bowl, combine the remaining ingredients; then stir into the dry mixture. Drop by the tablespoonful onto an oiled cookie sheet and bake for about 20-25 minutes until golden brown. Makes about 2 dozen.

FIG ROLL COOKIES

1 cup butter or soy margarine, melted
1/4 cup maple syrup
1 egg or equivalent egg replacer, beaten
1 tsp. vanilla extract
2 1/2-3 cups sifted flour (soy and rice or whole wheat)
1/8 tsp. sea salt
FIG WHIP p. 77

In a large bowl, combine the wet ingredients. Add the flour and salt; knead into a ball and chill well. Preheat the oven to 350°F. Roll out the dough to a 1/4-inch thickness and spread evenly with the FIG WHIP. Roll into a long cylinder and cut into 1-inch sections; place on an oiled cookie sheet and bake until lightly browned, about 20 minutes. Makes 2 dozen.

NUTTY COOKIES

2 cups each chopped cashews and pecans
2 cups oatmeal
6 Tbsp. carob powder
1/2 cup butter or soy margarine, melted
1 egg or equivalent egg replacer
1 tsp. vanilla extract
1/2 cup maple syrup

Combine the dry ingredients in a large mixing bowl. In another bowl, combine the wet ingredients; mix well and stir into the dry mixture. Drop by the teaspoonful onto oiled cookie sheets; bake at 350°F. for 20 minutes. Makes about 3 dozen.

OATMEAL-FRUIT BARS

1/2 cup butter or soy margarine, melted
1/4 cup maple syrup
1/4 cup apple juice concentrate
3 eggs or equivalent egg replacer
2 tsp. vanilla extract
2 1/2 cups oatmeal
1 cup flour (unbleached, whole wheat, soy, rice, etc.)
3 tsp. low-sodium baking powder
1/2 tsp. sea salt
1/2 cup chopped nuts
1/2 cup raisins
1 cup combined, chopped dried dates, apricots, and apples

Preheat the oven to 325°F. Combine the wet ingredients in a small bowl and set aside. In a large mixing bowl, combine the remaining ingredients; add the wet mixture and stir well. Spread in a rectangular baking pan and bake for 30-35 minutes. Cool before cutting into squares. Makes 3 dozen squares.

PEANUT BUTTER COOKIES

1/4 cup butter or soy margarine, melted
1/4-1/2 cup maple syrup
1 egg or equivalent egg replacer
1 cup PEANUT BUTTER p. 10
1/2 tsp. vanilla extract
1/2 tsp. sea salt (if unsalted peanut butter is used)
1/2 tsp. baking soda
2 cups soy flour

Preheat the oven to 375°F. In a large mixing bowl, combine the butter and the maple syrup; beat in the egg replacer, peanut butter, vanilla, salt and baking soda. Add the sifted flour and mix well. Roll the dough into 1-inch balls and place them on an oiled cookie sheet. Flatten them with a fork and bake for about 15 minutes. Makes about 2 dozen cookies.

RAISIN-SPICE COOKIES

1/2 cup butter or soy margarine
1/4 cup maple syrup
1/2 tsp. vanilla extract
1 egg or equivalent egg replacer
1 1/4 cups flour (rice, soy, unbleached, whole wheat)
1 cup oatmeal
1/4 tsp. sea salt
1/2 tsp. low-sodium baking powder
1/2 tsp. each ground cinnamon, ginger, cardamom
1/2 cup raisins
1/2 cup chopped nuts (pecans or walnuts)

Continued next page...

Preheat oven to 350°F. Melt the butter; add the maple syrup, egg or egg replacer and vanilla and beat until creamy. Sift the flour, salt, baking powder and spices together and stir into the butter mixture. Then stir in the raisins and nuts. (If the batter is too dry, stir in just a little NUT MILK p. 23.) Drop by the teaspoonful onto an oiled cookie sheet, about 1 inch apart. Bake for about 15 minutes or until golden brown. Makes about 1 1/2 dozen.

SAMA'S TEA COOKIES

20 dates, pitted
1/2 cup raisins
5 presoaked dried figs
1/2 cup water from soaked figs
1/2 cup butter or soy margarine, melted
1/4 cup maple syrup
3 eggs or equivalent egg replacer
2 tsp. vanilla extract
2 cups oatmeal
1 1/2 cups flour (unbleached, whole wheat, soy, rice)
1 Tbsp. low-sodium baking powder
1/2 tsp. sea salt

Preheat the oven to 325°F. Place the dates, raisins, figs and fig water in a blender or food processor and blend to a paste; set aside. Combine the wet ingredients in a small bowl. In a large mixing bowl, combine the dry ingredients; stir in the wet mixture. Drop by the heaping tablespoonful onto an oiled baking sheet; flatten to 1/2-inch thickness and spread the date mixture over the top. Bake for 20 minutes, until golden brown. Makes 1 dozen large cookies.

FROZEN DESSERTS

APPLE-CHERRY POPSICLES

Pour apple-cherry juice (found in the grocery store or made with 1 tsp. black cherry concentrate per glass of apple juice) into popsicle molds or an ice cube tray. (If using a tray, add the popsicle sticks when the liquid sets.) Freeze overnight or until solid and serve. Try other natural, unsweetened fruit juices (apple, grape, apricot, pineapple, etc.) for variety.

BANANA SHERBET

Peel overripe bananas (allow 1 banana per serving) and freeze overnight in a plastic bag. Chop into 1/2-inch pieces and blend in a food processor or blender until creamy. Add a little apple juice, if needed, to help blend. Serve in pretty parfait glasses with a strawberry, sprig of mint, slice of orange or nuts as a garnish.

FROZEN GRAPES, BANANAS AND STRAWBERRIES

Wash and stem a bunch of green seedless grapes and a pint of strawberries; dry on paper towels; place in a plastic bag and freeze. Peel and slice ripe bananas into 1-inch pieces; place in a plastic bag and freeze. Serve together, topped with BANANA SAUCE p. 181 or STRAWBERRY SAUCE p. 186 for a light dessert or separately as a snack.

MANGO ICE CREAM

4 large ripe mangoes
1 pint heavy whipping cream or thick CASHEW
    CREAM p. 182 or ALMOND CREAM p. 180

Peel and slice the mangoes; place in a plastic bag and freeze until solid. When ready to serve, whip up the cream and set aside. Place the frozen mangoes (cut into small chunks) in a food processor and blend until creamy. Add the cream; mix well and serve in parfait glasses with a sprig of fresh mint. Serves 8.

PAPAYA WITH FRUIT SHERBET

2 cups unsweetened pineapple juice
1/2 cup unsweetened apricot nectar
1/2 cup frozen unsweetened orange juice concentrate
2 ripe bananas
2 large ripe papayas
Shredded unsweetened coconut and fresh mint sprigs

Blend the fruit juices and bananas in a food processor until smooth; pour into a shallow container and freeze until almost firm, about 1 hour, stirring occasionally. Whisk the partially frozen mix a few seconds until smooth and slushy. Return to the shallow container and cover; freeze until firm. Allow the sherbet to sit at room temperature for 10-15 minutes before serving. Peel the papayas and slice in half; remove the seeds and cut into bite-sized slices. Fill individual bowls with the papaya slices and a scoop of sherbet; garnish with the coconut and fresh mint sprigs. Serves 8.

PINEAPPLE-STRAWBERRY SHERBET

2 cups crushed pineapple, drained
6 oz. unsweetened pineapple juice concentrate
1 pint of fresh strawberries, sliced
Fresh mint sprigs

Combine the pineapple and concentrate and blend until smooth; pour into a shallow container and freeze semi-hard. Whisk until smooth and slushy; fold in the sliced strawberries and freeze until firm. Garnish individual servings with fresh mint. Serves 4.

STRAWBERRY ICE CREAM

1 pint fresh strawberries
2 cups CASHEW CREAM p. 182 OR ALMOND CREAM p. 180

Wash and stem the strawberries; dry carefully and freeze in a plastic bag. Place the CASHEW or ALMOND CREAM in a shallow container and freeze. When ready to serve, blend together the cream and strawberries. Garnish individual servings with a whole strawberry or a sprig of fresh mint. Serves 4.

FRUIT DESSERTS

APPLE UPSIDE-DOWN CAKE

2 cups chopped apples
1 heaping tsp. cinnamon
1/2 cup raisins
1/2 cup chopped nuts
1 egg or equivalent egg replacer
2 Tbsp. butter or soy margarine
2 Tbsp. apple juice concentrate
2 Tbsp. maple syrup
1/2 cup milk or NUT MILK p. 23
1 Tbsp. low-sodium baking powder
1 1/4 cups unbleached wheat flour

Preheat the oven to 350°F. Mix the chopped apples, raisins, nuts and cinnamon together and place in the bottom of an oiled 8-inch square pan. Melt the butter and combine with the other wet ingredients; set aside. Sift the flour and baking powder together. Add the wet ingredients and mix well; pour over the apple mixture and bake for 30 minutes. Cool slightly and flip over onto a plate, apple side up. Pour warm APPLE SAUCE p. 180 on top and serve. (Follow the same procedure for individual cupcakes.) Serves 8.

BAKED APPLES

4 baking apples
2 Tbsp. butter or soy margarine
1 tsp. cinnamon
4 dried figs, chopped
8 dried apricots, chopped
1/2 cup raisins
1/4 cup apple juice concentrate
1/4 cup chopped walnuts

Wash and core the apples, leaving 1/2 inch at the bottom; set aside. Combine the remaining ingredients and mix well. Spoon the stuffing into the cored apples and bake at 350°F. until tender, about 30 minutes. Serves 4.

B R'S TROPICAL FRUIT COMPOTE

4 cups chopped sapodilla, seeded
1 cup chopped calamondin, seeded

In a blender or food processor combine the sapodilla and calamondin and blend until smooth; refrigerate and serve on toast, pancakes, yogurt, ice cream or as is. Sapodilla are _very_ sweet and calamondin are _very_ sour; both are available in tropical climates. Together they are a real treat! Makes about 3 cups.

CAROB-COATED FRESH FRUIT

CAROB COATING:
1/4 cup butter or soy margarine
1/4 cup maple syrup
6 Tbsp. carob powder
1/4 cup dairy, soy or NUT MILK p. 23
1/2 tsp. vanilla extract
A pinch of sea salt

FRUIT:
4 ripe bananas, peeled and cut into 1-inch pieces
1 cup finely ground peanuts, optional
    or
2 pints fresh strawberries
    or
Other fresh fruit of choice

Melt the butter in a small saucepan. Add the maple syrup, carob powder, milk and salt; mix well and simmer for about 5 minutes, stirring continuously. Add the vanilla and stir well; set aside to cool. Dip each piece of fruit into the cooled carob mixture until well coated; roll the bananas in the ground peanuts. Place on wax paper or a buttered platter to set. If the kitchen is too warm for the carob to set properly, place in the refrigerator or freezer until ready to serve as a snack or dessert. Serves 8.

DEEP-FRIED BANANAS

BATTER:
1/2 cup flour (chickpea, unbleached or whole wheat)
1 egg or equivalent egg replacer
2 Tbsp. PEANUT BUTTER p. 10
1/8 tsp. cinnamon
Water

FILLING:
3 bananas, cut into 1-inch pieces

Combine the batter ingredients and blend until smooth. Coat the banana pieces in the batter and deep-fry, a few at a time, until golden brown. Drain on paper towels and serve hot. Serves 6-8.

FIGS WITH CREAM

Dried figs (allow at least 3 figs per serving)
Whipping cream, CASHEW CREAM p. 182 or ALMOND
   CREAM p. 180

Fill a screw-top jar with dried figs and cover with water. Refrigerate for at least 24 hours before serving. Shake the jar occasionally to mix the liquid. The longer the figs soak, the thicker and sweeter the syrup becomes.

Just before serving, prepare the cream and use as a topping for individual servings of figs in their own syrup. Garnish with sprig of fresh mint and serve.

FIG WHIP

1 cup thick coconut milk or CASHEW
　　CREAM p. 182 or ALMOND CREAM p. 180
3 cups dried figs
1 Tbsp. ground sesame seeds
1 Tbsp. carob powder
2 Tbsp. raisins
1 tsp. fresh lemon juice, optional

Combine all the ingredients in a blender or food processor and blend until smooth; chill before serving. Spoon into fruit cups and garnish with a sprinkle of grated coconut. Or use as a filling for FIG ROLL COOKIES p. 66. Serves 6-8.

FRUIT "GELLO"

1/3 cup agar-agar flakes
1 cup orange juice
1 cup grape juice
1 cup crushed pineapple with juice

In a saucepan, dissolve the agar-agar flakes in the orange and grape juices and bring to a boil. Add the pineapple, reduce the heat and simmer for about 5 minutes, stirring continuously. Cool, then refrigerate until set. Top with sliced fresh fruit in season and thick ALMOND CREAM p. 180 OR CASHEW CREAM p. 182. (Experiment with your own juice combinations.) Serves 4.

FRUIT PLATTER

Arrange fresh fruits in season and assorted dried fruits and nuts attractively on a platter. (Include such fruit as fresh pineapple wedges, whole strawberries, papaya slices, grapes, peach slices, dried figs, dates, apricots.) Serve with TOFU-FRUIT DIP p. 12 or any other sweet dip. Garnish the fruit platter with fresh mint.

GEORGIAN FRUIT COMPOTE

3 cups mixed dried fruit (figs, raisins, apples apricots, prunes, etc.)
Cold water to cover fruit
2 Tbsp. potato starch or arrowroot
3/4 cup cooked BROWN RICE p. 132
Mace or cinnamon to taste
Fresh lemon juice to taste

Soak the dried fruit for at least 2 hours or overnight in cold water. Then stew them in the same water until soft, about 30 minutes. Add a touch of mace or cinnamon and simmer for 5 more minutes. Mix the potato starch or arrowroot with a little water and add to the fruit; mix in the rice and a squeeze of fresh lemon juice, if desired. Stir until thickened and serve plain or with cream, as a topping for pancakes or toast, or as a filling in pies or tarts. Makes about 4 cups.

PIE CRUSTS

ALMOND PIE CRUST

1 cup finely ground almonds
1 cup flour (unbleached, whole wheat, rice, soy)
2 Tbsp. butter or soy margarine
2 Tbsp. maple syrup
2 Tbsp. cold water (more if needed)

Combine all the ingredients; mix well and press into an oiled pie plate. Bake at 400°F. for 10-15 minutes. Fill with ALMOND-APRICOT CHEESECAKE p. 81, puddings, fresh fruit, etc. Makes 1 crust.

GRANOLA PIE CRUST

1 1/2 cups oatmeal
1/2 cup brown rice flour
1/2 cup currants
1/4 cup chopped dates
1/2 cup chopped pecans
3 Tbsp. shredded, unsweetened coconut
3 Tbsp. butter or soy margarine, melted

In a large bowl, mix together the oatmeal, flour, fruit and nuts. Stir in the butter and press into an 8-inch pie plate to form a crust. Bake at 350°F. for about 15 minutes until browned. Fill with PLUSH PECAN PIE p. 87 filling, fresh fruit, fruit compote or a pudding and serve. Makes 1 crust.

NUTTY TART SHELLS

2 cups ground pecans (or walnuts)
1/2 cup butter or soy margarine, melted

Mix the nuts and butter together well and press into tart pans, muffin tins or a pie plate. Bake at 350° F. for about 20 minutes, until crisp. Fill with SWEET POTATO TART p. 88 filling, DRIED FRUIT JAM p. 183, fresh fruit or pudding. Makes 10 tarts or 1 pie.

RICE FLOUR PIE CRUST

3 cups brown rice flour
1/2 tsp. cinnamon
1/2 cup butter or soy margarine, melted
1 cup ice cold water
1 tsp. vanilla extract

Preheat the oven to 400°F. Sift the flour and cinnamon together in a large bowl. Cut in the butter until crumbly. Add the vanilla and a little water; knead with your fingers. Add the remaining water until a ball is formed. Knead 1 minute more. Sprinkle a pastry sheet or waxed paper with a little flour. Roll out half the dough into a circle about 1/8-inch thick and turn over into a buttered pie plate. (Rice flour dough will be dry and crumbly compared to wheat.) If the dough breaks when turning into the pan, just pat it together with your fingers and proceed. Crimp the edges and puncture the sides and center with a fork. Bake for 15 minutes or until the crust is golden brown. Freeze the other half of the dough or make 2 pies. Makes 2 crusts.

PIES

ALMOND-APRICOT CHEESECAKE

CRUST: 1 ALMOND PIE CRUST p. 79, baked

FILLING:
1 1/2 lb. tofu
1/2 cup ALMOND MILK p. 16
1/2 cup maple syrup
1 tsp. vanilla extract
1/4 tsp. almond extract
1 Tbsp. lemon juice

Combine all the ingredients in a blender or food processor and blend until smooth. Pour into the crust and bake in a preheated oven at 325°F. for 30 minutes.

TOPPING:
1 cup dried apricots
2 cups apple juice or apricot nectar
1/2 cup raisins
1/4 tsp. cinnamon
1/4 cup shredded, unsweetened coconut

Combine all the ingredients in a saucepan and simmer for 30 minutes. Cool and place in a blender or food processor; blend until smooth. Pour as a topping over the tofu filling; chill well before serving. Serves 8.

APPLE COBBLER

6 cups sliced fresh apples
1 cup oatmeal
1/3 cup ground walnuts
1/4 cup brown rice flour
1 tsp. cinnamon
1/4 cup raisins
1/4 cup apple juice concentrate
1/4 tsp. fresh lemon juice

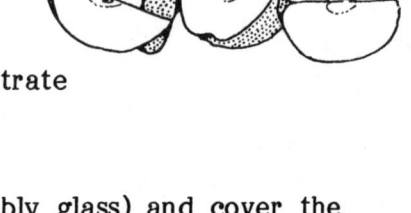

Butter a pie plate (preferably glass) and cover the bottom with the sliced apples. In a small bowl, combine the remaining ingredients and mix well; sprinkle over the apples. Dot with butter, if desired, and bake at 375°F. for 20-25 minutes or until the apples are soft. Serves 8.

BLUEBERRY-COCONUT CREAM PIE

1/2 cup frozen orange juice concentrate
1/4 tsp. ground cinnamon
2 pints fresh blueberries, or unsweetened frozen blueberries
1 Tbsp. potato starch, cornstarch or agar-agar flakes
1 baked and cooled 9-inch RICE FLOUR PIE CRUST p. 80
1 cup whipped cream or CASHEW CREAM p. 182
1/2 cup shredded, unsweetened coconut

Continued next page...

Combine the concentrate, cinnamon and half of the blueberries in a small saucepan; simmer until the berries pop open. Mash the berries; add the starch or agar-agar and simmer another 5 minutes, stirring constantly. Gently fold in the rest of the blueberries and pour into the baked crust. Cover and chill. When ready to serve, fold the coconut into the cream and pour on top of the blueberry filling. Garnish with a sprig of fresh mint and a few blueberries. Serves 8.

BLUEBERRY-MANGO PUDDING OR PIE

2 Tbsp. agar-agar flakes
1 pint blueberries
4 cups mango slices
1 cup whipped cream or CASHEW CREAM p. 182

Place the blueberries in a small pan and add the agar-agar and enough water to just cover the bottom of the pan; simmer, stirring continuously, until the berries have popped. Cool and blend in a food processor or blender until smooth; set aside. Meanwhile, simmer the mango slices with very little water until mushy; blend in the processor until smooth and gently fold in the cream.

FOR A PUDDING: Layer the mango and blueberry sauce in parfait glasses; garnish with mint. Serves 6.

FOR A PIE: Bake a RICE FLOUR PIE CRUST p. 80; cool and pour the mango cream into the crust. Then swirl the blueberry mixture into the mango; chill and garnish with fresh mint and blueberries. Serves 8.

CAROB CREME PIE

1 GRANOLA PIE CRUST p. 79, baked
2 ripe bananas, 1 sliced and 1 mashed
1 lb. tofu
1/2 cup plain yogurt or CASHEW CREAM p. 182
1/2 cup maple syrup
1 tsp. vanilla extract and 1/4 tsp. sea salt
6 Tbsp. carob powder
1/2 cup shredded, unsweetened coconut
Chopped walnuts for garnish

Cover the bottom of the crust with the sliced banana. Blend the remaining ingredients until smooth. Pour into the crust and top with the walnuts. Chill before serving. Serves 8.

CHERRY-TAPIOCA PUDDING OR PIE

1 16-oz. can pitted sour cherries, rinsed
2 Tbsp. each apple and black cherry concentrate
1/2 cup quick-cooking, granulated tapioca
1 1/2 cups apple juice
1/4 cup apple juice concentrate
1/4 cup black cherry concentrate
1/4 tsp. sea salt

In a small bowl, marinate the cherries in the 2 Tbsp. apple and black cherry concentrates. Place the remaining ingredients in a saucepan. Bring to a boil; reduce heat and simmer, stirring continuously for 10 minutes. Cool slightly; stir in the cherries with the marinade.

Continued next page...

FOR A PUDDING: Refrigerate the cherry mixture. When ready to serve, garnish with fresh mint and top with whipped cream or CASHEW CREAM p. 182. Serves 6-8.

FOR A PIE: Bake a RICE FLOUR PIE CRUST p. 80 Cool and fill with the cherry-tapioca mixture; top with whipped cream or CASHEW CREAM; chill. Serves 8.

FRESH FRUIT PIE

CRUST: 1 RICE FLOUR PIE CRUST p. 80, baked

FILLING:
1/2 cup frozen orange juice concentrate
1 cup pineapple juice
3 Tbsp. cornstarch, potato starch or agar-agar flakes
Maple syrup or other sweetener to taste, optional (try a few dried figs or dates, blended in the food processor with a little juice)
6 cups assorted fresh fruit, cut bite-sized — frozen, unsweetened fruit can also be used (raspberries, blueberries, strawberries, peaches, apples, pears, pineapple, etc)
Shredded, unsweetened coconut and fresh mint

In a small saucepan, heat the orange and pineapple juices. Add the starch or agar-agar and sweetener and stir until smooth and thick; remove from the heat and cool completely. Fold in the fresh fruit (drained) and turn into the baked crust. Garnish with coconut and fresh mint leaves. Serves 8.

VARIATION:
For the 6 cups fruit, try 2 cups blueberries, 3 cups mango slices, and 1 cup drained, crushed pineapple.

PEACH COBBLER

6 cups sliced fresh peaches and 1/2 cup peach nectar
1 cup oatmeal
1/3 cup ground pecans
1/4 cup brown rice flour
1 tsp. cinnamon
1/4 cup maple syrup
1/4 cup raisins

Butter a pie plate; cover the bottom with the peaches and nectar. Combine the oatmeal, pecans, flour, cinnamon and syrup and mix well; sprinkle on the peaches, dot with butter, if desired, and bake until the peaches are soft. Top with ALMOND CREAM p. 180. Serves 8.

PINEAPPLE-TAPIOCA PUDDING OR PIE

2 cups unsweetened pineapple juice
1/2 cup quick-cooking, granulated tapioca
1/8 tsp. ground ginger
1 cup crushed pineapple, drained
3 Tbsp. maple syrup
Pinch of sea salt, optional
1 tsp. vanilla extract
1 cup CASHEW CREAM p. 182

In a saucepan, combine all the ingredients except the vanilla and cream; bring to a boil, reduce the heat and simmer for about 10 minutes, stirring continuously. Set aside to cool; then stir in the vanilla and cream.

Continued next page...

FOR A PUDDING: Refrigerate and serve in individual dishes with a garnish of fresh mint. Serves 6.

FOR A PIE: Bake a RICE FLOUR PIE CRUST p. 80 or a GRANOLA PIE CRUST p. 79; cool and fill with the pineapple-tapioca mixture. Chill well and garnish with fresh mint. Serves 8.

PLUSH PECAN PIE

CRUST: 1 GRANOLA PIE CRUST p. 79, baked

FILLING:
1/4 cup quick-cooking, granulated tapioca
1 cup apple juice
1/4 cup maple syrup
1/4 cup butter or soy margarine
1 tsp. vanilla extract
2 cups pecan halves or pieces

Place the tapioca and apple juice in a saucepan and cook on medium heat, stirring continuously, for about 5 minutes; the mixture should be fairly thick. Add the maple syrup and butter and stir until the butter is melted. Add the vanilla and pecans and mix until the pecans are well coated. Pour into the baked crust; bake at 350°F. for 15 minutes. Cool and serve with ALMOND or CASHEW CREAM p. 180 or 182. Serves 8.

SWEET POTATO TARTS

CRUST: 10 NUTTY TART SHELLS p. 80, unbaked

FILLING:
2 cups cooked sweet potatoes
1/2 cup stock from potatoes (more to thin,
   if necessary)
1 egg or equivalent egg replacer
3 Tbsp. orange juice concentrate
1 tsp. ground cinnamon
1/2 tsp. ground ginger
1/2 tsp. ground cloves
1/2 tsp. ground allspice
1 tsp. vanilla extract
1/2 tsp. sea salt
1/2 cup raisins
ALMOND CREAM p. 180 or CASHEW CREAM p. 182
Shredded, unsweetened coconut

Mash or blend the sweet potatoes until smooth. Add the remaining ingredients except the cream and coconut and mix well. Spoon into the shells and bake at 350°F. for 30 minutes. Cool and serve. Top with ALMOND or CASHEW CREAM and shredded coconut. Makes 10 tarts.

Entrees

Acorn Squash with
  Tofu Stuffing, 90
Andrea's Vegetarian
  Chili, 91
Asparagus Crepes, 92
Bean Burrito, 92
Black Bean Pie, 93
Black Beans with Soy
  "Sausage," 94
Dried Beans, 94
Falafel, 96
Individual Spinach
  "Quiches," 97
Lasagna, 98
Laurie's Broccoli-Cauli-
  flower Casserole, 98
Lemon-Ginger Tofu, 99
Lentil-Stuffed
  Cabbage, 100
Lentil-Vegie Loaf, 101
Marinated Tofu, 102
Mexican Garbanzos, 104
Mexican Tofu, 104
Nutty Spinach Pie, 105
Oriental Tofu, 106
Pizza Supreme, 107
Rice-Stuffed Cabbage, 108
Russian Cabbage Pie, 110
Shepherd's Pie, 111

Soy "Sausage," 112
Spaghetti Squash
  Casserole, 113
Spaghetti with Soy
  "Sausage," 113
Szechuan Salad, 114
Tofu Burgers, 115
Tofu Creole, 116
Tofu Croquettes, 117
Tofu Egg(less)
  Salad I, 118
Tofu Egg(less)
  Salad II, 118
Tofu Egg(less)
  Salad III, 119
Tofu Fritters, 119
Tofu Kebabs, 120
Tofu-Mushroom
  Stroganoff, 120
Tofu Roast, 122
Tofu Sloppy Joes, 123
Tofu Steak, 123
Tofu Tetrazzini, 124
Tofu Turkey, 125
Tofu-Vegetable Stew, 126
Tofu with Walnuts, 126
Vegetable Enchiladas, 127
Vegetable-Stuffed
  Tofu, 128

ACORN SQUASH WITH TOFU STUFFING

3 acorn squash
1 lb. tofu
3/4 cup brown rice flour
1/2 tsp. sea salt and pepper to taste
1 medium onion, or 6-8 green onions, chopped
1 large red or green bell pepper, chopped
1/3 cup chopped fresh parsley
1 cup cooked MILLET p. 137
1/2 cup chopped walnuts
1/2 cup HOT TACO SAUCE p. 189

STUFFING:
In a large bowl, crumble the tofu. Add the rice flour, salt and pepper and toss until the tofu is well coated with flour. Place the mixture in a heated frying pan with enough oil to cover the bottom. Fry on medium-high heat for about 45 minutes, until the tofu is very crisp and golden brown; stir frequently. Add the onions and bell peppers; sauté until tender. Add the parsley, millet, walnuts and hot sauce and mix well.

SQUASH:
Wash and cut the acorn squash in half; remove the seeds and place in a large steamer. Steam until almost done but still firm; remove from the heat, uncover, and set aside. Spoon the stuffing into the center of each squash half; place in a large baking dish or pan with a little water in the bottom. Bake at 350°F. for about 30 minutes or until the squash is soft. Garnish with tomato wedges and parsley sprigs. Serves 6.

ANDREA'S VEGETARIAN CHILI

2 Tbsp. oil
1 1/2 cups chopped celery
1 1/2 cups chopped green pepper
1 cup chopped onion
3 cloves garlic, minced
2 28-oz. cans tomatoes, chopped or 8 cups chopped fresh tomatoes
6 cups red kidney beans
1/4 cup cider or rice vinegar
2 Tbsp. chili powder (more to taste)
2 Tbsp. chopped fresh parsley
2 tsp. sea salt
1 1/2 tsp. dried or 1 Tbsp. fresh basil
1 tsp. dried or 2 tsp. fresh oregano
1 1/2 tsp. ground cumin
1/4 tsp. freshly ground pepper
1/4 tsp. cayenne pepper, optional
1 bay leaf
1/4 cup butter or soy margarine
1 cup textured vegetable protein (soy granules)

In a large pot, sauté the celery, peppers, onion and garlic in the oil until tender. Stir in the remaining ingredients and simmer for 1 1/2 hours. Serve with rice. (It's even better the next day, so prepare ahead, if possible.) Serves 8 with leftovers.

ASPARAGUS CREPES

24 fresh asparagus spears
WATERCRESS SAUCE p. 195
8 WHOLE WHEAT CREPES p. 40

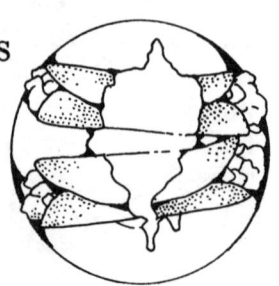

To prepare the asparagus for cooking: hold the stem and the tip ends between the fingertips of each hand. Bend the asparagus until it breaks. Discard the stem ends and steam the tips until tender-crisp. Prepare the WATERCRESS SAUCE and the WHOLE WHEAT CREPES. Place 3 asparagus spears in the center of each crepe and spoon on 2 Tbsp. of the WATERCRESS SAUCE. Roll the crepes and arrange them, side by side, in a baking dish; top with the remaining sauce and bake in a preheated oven at 400°F. for about 10 minutes. Serve immediately. Serves 4.

BEAN BURRITO

2 Tbsp. oil
1 onion, chopped
4 cups cooked kidney or pinto beans
1 tsp. ground cumin
1 clove garlic, minced or 1/8 tsp. garlic powder
1 tsp. chili powder
1/2 cup HOT TACO SAUCE p. 189
Sea salt and pepper to taste
12 flour tortillas
Cheese, optional
MEXICAN TOMATO SAUCE p. 191

Continued next page...

Heat the oil in a large skillet and sauté the onion until tender; add the garlic, chili powder and hot sauce. Purée the beans in a food processor or blender and add to the skillet. Mix well and cook on medium heat, stirring every few minutes until the liquid is absorbed and the beans thicken into a paste. Separate the flour tortillas and fill them with the bean paste. Fold the tortillas around the beans as if making an envelope (all ends tucked in); place, flap down, on a serving dish. Top with cheese and the MEXICAN TOMATO SAUCE, reheat for about 10 minutes in a preheated oven at 400° F. and serve immediately. Makes 12 burritos.

BLACK BEAN PIE

CRUST: 1 TOFU FRITTER p. 119 recipe

FILLING:
1 medium onion, chopped
4-6 green chilies or 1 green bell pepper, chopped
6 cups cooked black beans
1 cup HOT TACO SAUCE p. 189
4 leaves cilantro (fresh coriander), optional
1 tsp. ground cumin

Oil and flour a pie plate or shallow baking dish. Form the TOFU FRITTER mix into a crust and bake at 350°F. for 1 hour or until golden brown. In a large skillet, sauté the onion and peppers in a little oil, until tender; add the beans, hot sauce, cilantro and cumin. Simmer, stirring frequently, until the mixture thickens; pour into the baked crust. Bake at 350°F. for about 20 minutes and serve with rice. Serves 6-8.

BLACK BEANS WITH SOY "SAUSAGE"

1/2 cup each chopped onion and green pepper
1 garlic clove, minced
1 cup SOY "SAUSAGE" p. 112, crumbled
3 small yellow squash, cut into bite-sized pieces
2 medium tomatoes, coarsely chopped
1/2 tsp. dried or 1 tsp. fresh minced oregano
2 cups cooked black beans
1/2 cup vegetable stock
1/2 tsp. sea salt and freshly ground pepper to taste
2 cups cooked BROWN RICE p. 132

In a large skillet, heat a little oil and sauté the onion, green pepper and garlic until tender. Add the SOY "SAUSAGE" and sauté until browned. Add the remaining ingredients except the rice; mix well, cover and simmer for about 10 minutes. Add the rice, toss gently and serve. Serves 4.

DRIED BEANS

When cooking dried beans, a pressure cooker conserves much time and energy. If you don't own a pressure cooker, follow the cooking instructions on the package.

To pressure-cook dried beans, the following general rules are important to keep in mind:

1. Allow 6 cups water to 2 cups dried beans and 2 Tbsp. oil (the oil coats the surface, preventing loose bean skins from clogging the steam vent).

Continued next page...

2. If the steam vent clogs, remove the cooker from the heat and release the pressure; open and clean out the vent pipe. Then resume cooking.
3. Never fill the pressure cooker over 1/2 full.
4. DO NOT pressure-cook split peas, as they produce a foam which clogs up the steam vent.
5. Always follow the instructions in your pressure cooker manual.

Presoaking overnight and rinsing well before cooking substantially cuts down on the cooking time and the digestibility of the beans. If presoaking in a warm kitchen, refrigerate so that the beans will not sour or ferment. Skim off the floating skins prior to cooking. To make a bean gravy, add more water, if necessary, to cover the beans and continue cooking for 15-30 minutes longer without the lid. Season to taste and add vegetables or use in other recipes.

Pressure cooking times for commonly used beans are listed in the following table:

Name of dried bean	Pressure cooking times soaked	unsoaked
Black beans	35 min.	45–50 min.
Black-eyed peas	20 min.	30 min.
Garbanzo beans (chickpeas)	30 min.	1 hr.–1 hr., 15 min.
Great Northern beans	10-12 min.	30 min.
Kidney beans	25-30 min.	1 hr.–1 hr., 15 min.
Lentils	20 min.	30 min.
Lima beans	25 min.	1 hr.–1 hr., 15 min.
Navy beans	10-12 min.	25 min.
Pink beans	30 min.	1 hr.–1 hr., 15 min.
Pinto beans	25-30 min.	1 hr.–1 hr., 15 min.
Soybeans	30-40 min.	45 min.–1 hr.

FALAFEL

3 cups cooked garbanzo beans (chickpeas)
1/2 cup cooked BROWN RICE p. 132
1 cooked potato
1/3 cup tahini
Vegetable stock, as needed
1 medium onion, chopped
2 cloves garlic, minced
1/2 cup brown rice flour
2 Tbsp. chopped fresh parsley
3 tsp. ground cumin
2 Tbsp. lemon juice
Sea salt and pepper to taste

Purée the beans, rice, potato and tahini in a food processor; add a little vegetable stock, if necessary, to blend. Combine the remaining ingredients and mix well; add to the bean mixture and blend. Form into 1-inch balls or small patties; fry in a non-stick skillet over medium heat until crisp on all sides or bake at 350°F. on an oiled baking sheet for 30 minutes. Serve as an entrée with rice and vegetables or as a pita bread sandwich with MIDDLE EASTERN SLAW p. 158 and TAHINI SAUCE p. 195. Serves 4-6.

INDIVIDUAL SPINACH "QUICHES"

CRUST:
RICE FLOUR PIE CRUST dough p. 80

Prepare the RICE FLOUR PIE CRUST dough as directed, omitting the vanilla and cinnamon. Divide the dough into 24 small balls and press each ball into an oiled muffin cup, forming miniature pie crusts. Bake at 350°F. for 10-15 minutes or until golden brown.

FILLING:
1/4 cup butter or soy margarine
6 green onions, sliced
3 lb. fresh or frozen spinach, chopped
3 Tbsp. egg replacer whipped (extra thick) with 6 Tbsp. water
1/2 lb. tofu
1/2 cup CASHEW CREAM p. 182
1 Tbsp. tamari or liquid soy protein
1/4 tsp. nutmeg or mace
1/2 tsp. sea salt
Pepper to taste

In a large skillet, sauté the green onions in the butter, add the spinach, cover and simmer until tender. In a food processor, blend the remaining ingredients and stir into the spinach mixture. Spoon into the muffin tin crusts and bake at 350°F. for about 20 minutes. Remove from the oven and set aside for 5 minutes before removing from the tins. Serve with a tomato salad. Makes 24 "quiches."

LASAGNA

1 pkg. lasagna noodles (Jerusalem artichoke or whole wheat noodles) or BROWN RICE p. 132
TOFU "RICOTTA CHEESE" p. 148
MUSHROOM-SOY PASTA SAUCE p. 192

Cook the lasagna noodles as directed on the package. Oil a large baking dish and layer the noodles, "cheese" and sauce. (BROWN RICE can be layered in place of the noodles.) Repeat the layering until the dish is filled. Bake at 350°F. about 30 minutes until the sauce bubbles. Serves 8.

LAURIE'S BROCCOLI-CAULIFLOWER CASSEROLE

TOFU BURGER p. 115 recipe or BROWN RICE p. 132
TOFU "RICOTTA CHEESE" p. 148
1 head of broccoli
1 head of cauliflower
4 Tbsp. butter or soy margarine
3 Tbsp. liquid soy protein or tamari
2 Tbsp. powdered vegetable broth
1/2 tsp. sea salt and freshly ground pepper to taste
1/4 cup minced parsley

Oil a large baking dish. Form the TOFU BURGER mixture into a crust about 1/2-inch thick; bake at 350°F. for 30-40 minutes until browned. Or press BROWN RICE into a crust 1-inch thick and set aside.

Continued next page...

Prepare the TOFU "RICOTTA CHEESE" and set aside. Wash the cauliflower and broccoli and cut into bite-sized pieces; steam lightly. In a large skillet, melt the butter; add the seasonings and cauliflower and broccoli pieces and sauté for 5 minutes, stirring frequently. Add the "cheese" and mix well. Pour into the crust and sprinkle with minced parsley. Bake in a preheated oven at 350°F. for 20 minutes. Serves 8.

LEMON-GINGER TOFU

1/2 cup tamari
1/4 cup sherry or wine
1/4 cup crushed pineapple
2 tsp. cornstarch, potato starch or arrowroot
2 lb. tofu, sliced into thin strips
3 Tbsp. oil and 1 Tbsp. toasted sesame oil
Peel of 1 lemon, grated
1/2 cup finely sliced white onion
4 stalks celery, sliced
1 lb. mushrooms, sliced
1 8-oz. can water chestnuts, sliced
2 tsp. ground or 1 Tbsp. grated fresh ginger
1 cup vegetable stock
Lemon slices

In a bowl, combine the tamari, sherry, pineapple and starch or arrowroot; stir in the tofu until well coated. Marinate for 15 minutes; then bake at 350°F. for 30 minutes. Heat the oils in a large skillet or wok; stir-fry the lemon peel, onion and celery for about 2 minutes. Add the mushrooms, water chestnuts, ginger and vegetable stock; bring to a boil, stirring continuously. Add the cooked tofu; stir-fry 2 minutes. Serve at once with rice; garnish with lemon slices. Serves 8.

LENTIL-STUFFED CABBAGE

1 large head cabbage

STUFFING:
2 cups cooked lentils
3 cups cooked BROWN RICE p. 132
1 tsp. dried or 1 Tbsp. fresh minced basil
3 Tbsp. miso (diluted with vegetable or lentil stock)
2 Tbsp. powdered vegetable broth
1 tsp. paprika or 1/2 sweet red pepper, chopped and sautéed
1/2 onion, chopped and sautéed
1 cup chopped walnuts

SAUCE:
1 pint MOCK or LOW-FAT "SOUR CREAM" p. 145-6
1 cup vegetable stock
1 tsp. paprika
1 tsp. dill
1 Tbsp. tamari

Wash and core the cabbage; place in a large pot and steam until the leaves are tender and can be easily pulled off the head. Cool and separate the leaves; set aside. Combine all the stuffing ingredients in a large bowl and mix well; place a couple of tablespoonsful on each leaf toward the stem. Then fold over each side and roll toward the leafy edge. Place the stuffed leaves, seam down, in a large, oiled baking dish. Sprinkle with tamari and set aside. Combine all the sauce ingredients and blend well; pour over the stuffed leaves and bake at 350°F. for 30 minutes. Serves 8.

LENTIL-VEGIE LOAF

1/2 cup chopped onion
2 stalks celery, chopped
1/2 large organic carrot, chopped
1 large green or red pepper, chopped
2 small tomatoes, chopped
2 cups cooked BROWN RICE p. 132
1 1/2 cups bread crumbs (10 slices)
1/2 cup chopped walnuts
2 cups cooked lentils
1/4 cup chopped green olives, optional
2 tsp. herb seasoning salt or 1 tsp. sea salt
2 tsp. powdered vegetable broth
2 eggs or equivalent egg replacer

In a large skillet, sauté the onion, celery, carrot, pepper and tomatoes until tender. Combine the sautéed vegetables and the remaining ingredients and mix well. Form into a loaf and bake in an oiled loaf pan for about 45 minutes at 350°F. Or form into burgers and bake or fry. Serve with rice and a gravy or sauce. Serves 6-8.

MARINATED TOFU

The marinade suggestions in this section will provide enough liquid to cover 1 pound of tofu cut into small cubes or slices. Combine the ingredients of the chosen marinade and mix well. Pour over the tofu and chill for several hours, tossing gently every 30 minutes or so. When ready to cook, drain the marinade and set it aside to use later as a sauce. Then cook the tofu:

1. Stir-fry with vegetables;

2. Bake at 350°F. for 30 minutes, until firm and browned;

3. Broil for several minutes on each side;

4. Skewer with vegetables, as a kebab and barbecue;

5. Combine with vegetables and/or grains in a casserole.

To prepare the marinade as a heated sauce, add an appropriate liquid (vegetable stock, NUT MILK p. 23, fruit or vegetable juice, etc.) to dilute the strength of the marinade, if necessary. Set aside 1/2 cup of the diluted liquid; heat the remaining liquid to a boil. Reduce the heat and add the 1/2 cup mixed with 1 Tbsp. arrowroot, potato starch or cornstarch for each cup of marinade; stir continuously until thickened.
Serve with the cooked tofu over rice and/or vegetables. Serves 2-4.

Continued next page...

SUGGESTED MARINADES:

1. 1/4 cup chopped green onions
   1/2 tsp. grated fresh ginger
   1/8 tsp. cayenne pepper
   Pinch garlic powder
   1/2 cup tamari
   1/2 cup vegetable stock

2. 1/2 cup vegetable stock
   1/4 cup TOFU MAYONNAISE p. 147
   1/4 cup lemon juice
   1 garlic clove, minced
   1/2 tsp. dried dill weed
   Sea salt and pepper to taste

3. 1 cup tomato juice
   2 Tbsp. tamari
   1/4 tsp. Tabasco® sauce
   1 tsp. PEANUT BUTTER p. 10
   1 Tbsp. lemon juice
   1 tsp. apple juice concentrate
   1/2 cup pineapple juice

4. 1/2 cup vegetable stock
   2 Tbsp. miso
   1/4 cup chopped green onions with tops
   1 tsp. grated fresh ginger
   1 clove garlic, minced
   1/4 cup fresh lemon juice
   1 Tbsp. grated lemon peel
   2 Tbsp. sherry or wine
   1 Tbsp. apple juice concentrate
   1 Tbsp. oil
   1/8 tsp. cayenne pepper

Also see Salad Dressings and Sauces for other good marinades.

MEXICAN GARBANZOS

1 medium onion, chopped
1 clove garlic, minced
1 stalk celery, chopped
1 green pepper, chopped
3 Tbsp. oil
1 cup cooked garbanzo beans
1 16-oz. can crushed tomatoes
1/2 tsp. oregano
1/2 tsp. basil
1/2 tsp. ground cumin
1/4 tsp. chili powder
Salt to taste

In a large skillet, sauté the vegetables in the oil until tender; add the beans, tomatoes with their juice and the seasonings. Place in a casserole dish and bake in a preheated oven at 350°F. for 45 minutes. Serves 4-6.

MEXICAN TOFU

Oil
2 lb. tofu, thinly sliced
1 medium onion, chopped
2 small green peppers, chopped
2-3 cups HOT TACO SAUCE p. 189
Sea salt and pepper to taste

Continued next page...

Cover the bottom of a large skillet with oil (use 2 to save time). Fry the tofu until golden brown on both sides; remove and drain on paper towels. Sauté the onion and green pepper until tender in the remaining oil; add the hot sauce and the tofu. Adjust the seasoning and simmer for a few minutes to blend the flavors. Serve with rice. Serves 8.

VARIATION:
Add 2 cups of SPICY VEGETABLE SOUP p. 210 at the end and simmer for 5 minutes to blend the flavors.

NUTTY SPINACH PIE

TOFU BURGER p. 115 recipe
TOFU "RICOTTA CHEESE" p. 148
3 lb. fresh or frozen spinach, chopped
1/4 cup butter or soy margarine
1/2 onion, chopped
1 cup chopped walnuts or pine nuts
Sea salt or tamari and pepper to taste

Mix the ingredients for the burger recipe; press into 3 pie plates or muffin tins for a 1/2-inch-thick crust. Bake at 350°F. for 30-40 minutes, until browned and firm to the touch. Meanwhile, cook the spinach, drain well and place in a large mixing bowl. Prepare the TOFU "RICOTTA CHEESE" and stir into the spinach. Sauté the onions in the butter and add, with the walnuts, to the spinach mixture. Season to taste. Fill the baked crusts and return to the 350°F. oven for 20 minutes or until bubbly. Makes 3 large pies or 36 muffin-sized pies.

ORIENTAL TOFU

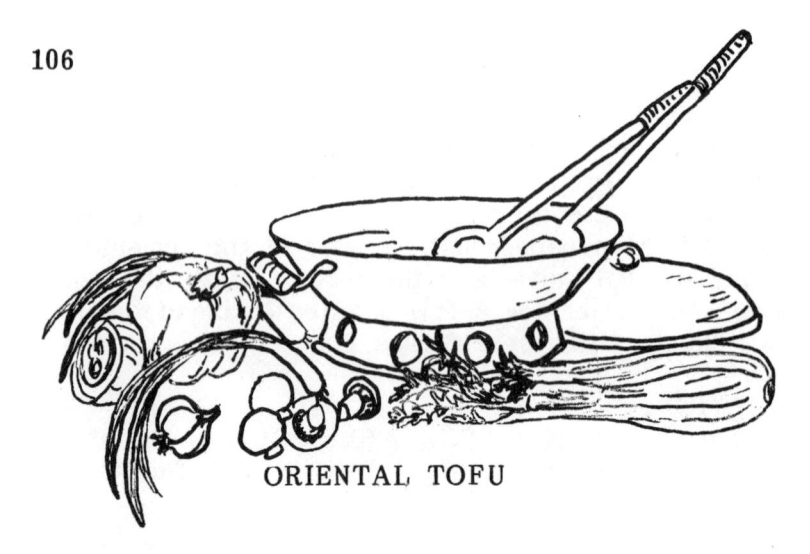

2 lb. tofu
3/4 cup liquid soy protein or 1/2 cup tamari
8 green onions and tops, sliced
2 Tbsp. toasted sesame oil
2 Tbsp. oil
1/8 tsp. cayenne pepper, optional
1/2 tsp. ground ginger or 1 tsp. grated fresh ginger
1/2 lb. Chinese pea pods (snow peas), fresh or frozen
1/2 lb. fresh mushrooms, sliced
1 8-oz. can water chestnuts, sliced
1 1/2 cups cold vegetable stock
2 Tbsp. cornstarch, potato starch or arrowroot

Cut the tofu into 1/2-inch cubes and marinate in the liquid soy protein or tamari for 15-20 minutes; basting frequently. Meanwhile, place the green onions, mushrooms and water chestnuts in a large skillet or wok with the oils, cayenne pepper and ginger. Stir-fry until tender-crisp; add the pea pods, tofu and marinade and stir-fry another 5 minutes. Dissolve the starch or arrowroot in the cold vegetable stock and add to the tofu mixture, stirring continuously, until thickened. Adjust the seasoning and serve over rice noodles. Serves 4-6.

PIZZA SUPREME

CRUST:
TOFU BURGER p. 115 recipe

Oil 2 pie plates (or muffin tins for mini pizzas) and shape the tofu mixture into crusts about 1/2-inch thick. Bake at 350°F. for about 35-40 minutes until golden brown and firm to the touch.

TOPPING:
1 medium onion, sliced
2-3 red or green bell peppers, sliced
1 lb. fresh mushrooms, sliced
3 yellow or zucchini squash, sliced, optional
Sea salt or herb seasoning salt to taste
ITALIAN TOMATO SAUCE p. 190
Grated mild, white, rennetless cheese, optional

In a large skillet, sauté the onion, peppers, mushrooms and squash in vegetable oil until tender-crisp; season to taste. Cover the bottom of the precooked crusts with the ITALIAN TOMATO SAUCE and layer with the sautéed vegetables. Top with the grated cheese, if desired, and bake at 350°F. about 20 minutes to blend the flavors and melt the cheese. Makes two 9-inch pizzas or 24 mini pizzas.

RICE-STUFFED CABBAGE

CABBAGE LEAVES:
Core a head of cabbage so that the outer leaves separate easily; steam for about 10-15 minutes until tender. Carefully peel off the leaves and blanch in boiling water for 5 minutes; drain. Plunge into cold water and fill with stuffing.

STUFFING:
1 cup textured vegetable protein (soy granules)
1 cup vegetable stock or water
1 small onion, chopped
1/4 cup oil
1 1/2-2 cups cooked BROWN RICE p. 132
2 Tbsp. chopped fresh parsley
1 tsp. paprika
1/8 tsp. garlic powder
1/8 tsp. basil or thyme
1/8 tsp. cayenne pepper
Sea salt to taste
1 cup chopped walnuts

Soak the textured vegetable protein in the vegetable stock or water and set aside. Sauté the onion; add the textured vegetable protein and the remaining ingredients. Mix well and adjust the seasoning to taste. Spoon the stuffing onto each cabbage leaf at the stem end and fold into a closed packet; place close together, seam down, in an oiled baking dish and dot with butter.

Continued next page...

SAUCE:
2 cups or more stewed tomatoes
1/2 cup chopped onion
2 Tbsp. butter or soy margarine
1/2 tsp. basil
1/8 tsp. garlic powder
1/2 tsp. paprika
1/8 tsp. cayenne pepper
Squeeze of fresh lemon
1/2 cup or more dairy or MOCK "SOUR
    CREAM" p. 146
Tamari or sea salt to taste

Combine all the sauce ingredients in a food processor and purée. Pour the sauce over the cabbage rolls and bake at 350°F. until the leaves are tender and sauce is bubbly (about 45 minutes). Serves 6-8.

RUSSIAN CABBAGE PIE

3 cups cooked BROWN RICE p. 132
4 Tbsp. butter or soy margarine
1/2 cup chopped onion
1 head cabbage, shredded
1/8 tsp. tarragon
1/8 tsp. basil
1/8 tsp. marjoram
Sea salt and pepper to taste
1 lb. mushrooms, sliced
2 Tbsp. tamari
1/4 cup lemon juice
1 TOFU MAYONNAISE p. 147 recipe
Chopped dill weed

Oil the sides and bottom of a large baking dish. Press the cooked rice into a crust about 1-inch thick and set aside. In a large skillet, melt 2 Tbsp. of the butter and sauté the onion and cabbage for about 5 minutes; add the tarragon, basil, marjoram, salt and pepper. Cover and simmer until tender; set aside. Melt the remaining butter and sauté the mushrooms until tender; add the tamari and lemon juice and set aside. Prepare the TOFU MAYONNAISE and spread half of it over the rice crust; sprinkle with dill. Next make a layer of the cabbage mix, followed by a layer of the mushrooms. Top with the rest of the TOFU MAYONNAISE and bake at 400°F. for 30 minutes. Serves 4-6.

SHEPHERD'S PIE

1 uncooked RICE FLOUR PIE CRUST p. 80
6 medium potatoes, diced
2 carrots, diced
2 cups cooked Great Northern beans
1/2-1 cup GRAVY I or II p. 188
2 cups cooked field peas or black-eyed peas
1 cup cooked lima beans
1/2 tsp. basil
1/4 tsp. marjoram
1/4 cup tamari or 1/3 cup liquid soy protein
A little milk, soy milk or NUT MILK p. 23
2 Tbsp. butter or soy margarine
Sea salt and pepper to taste

Prepare 1 crust and set aside, unbaked. (Freeze the remaining dough for use later or make a FRESH FRUIT PIE p. 85 for dessert.) Steam the diced potatoes and carrots, placing the carrots over to one side, so that some potatoes can later be removed to mash for the topping. Meanwhile, combine the Great Northern beans and gravy in a food processor or blender; process until smooth. Combine the bean mixture in a large bowl with the field peas, lima beans, basil, marjoram, and tamari; mix well.

When the potatoes and carrots are tender, remove 2 1/2 cups of potatoes and blend with a little milk, butter, salt and pepper to make a mashed potato topping; set aside. Add the remaining potatoes and carrots to the bean mixture; stir well and pour into the pie crust. Spread the mashed potatoes over the top and bake in a preheated oven at 350°F. for about 45 minutes, until the crust and topping are lightly browned. (Prepare hours ahead and bake just before serving.) Serves 6-8.

SOY "SAUSAGE"

1/2 cup tomato sauce
1/2 cup vegetable stock
1 tsp. powdered vegetable broth
2 Tbsp. oil
1 cup textured vegetable protein (soy granules)
2 eggs or equivalent egg replacer
1 tsp. Tabasco® sauce
Cayenne pepper to taste
1/2 tsp. sea salt
1/2 cup toasted bread crumbs
1/2 cup chopped green onions
1/2 cup chopped celery
1/4 cup rice flour

Combine the tomato sauce, powdered broth, vegetable stock and oil; stir in the textured vegetable protein and set aside to soak. Whisk the egg or egg replacer, Tabasco® sauce, salt, and cayenne pepper together in a large bowl; stir in the bread crumbs and let stand for a few minutes. Add the onions, celery, flour and soaked textured vegetable protein and work together with your hands or a fork until thoroughly blended. Adjust the seasoning to taste and use in recipes calling for ground beef or sausage. Serves 4.

TO MAKE PATTIES OR "SAUSAGE" BALLS:
Form into the desired shape and fry until browned, or bake at 350°F. for about 35-40 minutes.

TO MAKE A LOAF:
Shape into a loaf and bake in an oiled loaf pan at 350°F. for 1 hour.

SPAGHETTI SQUASH CASSEROLE

SPAGHETTI SQUASH p. 226
MUSHROOM SOY-PASTA SAUCE p. 192
TOFU "RICOTTA CHEESE" p. 148

Prepare the above recipes as directed. Repeat layers of the squash, "cheese" and sauce in a large, oiled baking dish; bake at 350°F. until bubbly, about 30 minutes. Serves 6-8.

SPAGHETTI WITH SOY "SAUSAGE"

1 pkg. spaghetti or linguini (whole wheat, Jerusalem artichoke or rice flour)
ITALIAN TOMATO SAUCE p. 190
SOY "SAUSAGE" balls p. 112

Prepare the spaghetti and the sauce and "sausage" recipes as directed. Place the cooked pasta in the bottom of a large serving bowl; pour on the sauce and make a ring around the center with the "sausage" balls. Garnish with fresh parsley and serve with a large vegetable salad. Serves 6-8.

SZECHUAN SALAD

1/2 cup lemon juice or cider or rice vinegar
1/4 cup tamari or low-sodium soy sauce
Crushed, dried hot peppers or cayenne pepper to taste
1 garlic clove, minced
1/2 tsp. grated fresh ginger
1/2 lb. tofu, thinly sliced
16 bamboo shoot slices
4 water chestnuts, sliced
1/2 cup vegetable stock
1 tsp. powdered vegetable broth
2 cups broccoli flowerettes
1 sweet red bell pepper, cut into strips
1 cup sliced fresh mushrooms

Combine the lemon juice, tamari, hot pepper, garlic and ginger; mix well, and use as a marinade for the sliced tofu, bamboo shoots and water chestnuts. Refrigerate and toss occasionally. Meanwhile, dissolve the powdered vegetable broth in the vegetable stock. In a large, non-stick skillet, heat about half of this liquid. Add the broccoli and stir-fry until tender-crisp. Remove the broccoli and set aside. Add a little more broth if needed and stir-fry the red pepper strips in the same pan over medium heat until just tender; remove and add to the broccoli. Stir-fry the mushrooms and add to the broccoli mix. Add the marinated tofu, bamboo shoots and water chestnuts to the vegetable mixture and toss gently. Cover and chill for several hours or overnight before serving. Serve with chilled brown rice on lettuce for a cool summer meal. Serves 4.

TOFU BURGERS

2 lb. tofu
1 medium onion, chopped
1/2 lb. carrots, grated
1/2-1 cup HOT TACO SAUCE p. 189
1/4 tsp. basil
1/2-1 tsp. sea salt
1 cup finely chopped roasted peanuts
1/4 cup chopped fresh parsley
1 egg or equivalent egg replacer
1 cup brown rice flour

In a large mixing bowl, crumble the tofu and set aside. Sauté the onions in a little oil and add to the tofu. Add the remaining ingredients and mix very well. Form into patties and fry until browned and crisp on both sides, or bake at 350°F. until firm and browned, about 30 minutes. Serve the burgers with rice, vegetables and a sauce or on pita bread with sliced vegetables. Makes about 12 burgers.

VARIATIONS:
Use the uncooked mixture as a crust for PIZZA SUPREME p. 107, NUTTY SPINACH PIE p. 105 or your own vegetable pies.

TOFU CREOLE

2 Tbsp. butter or soy margarine
1/4 cup chopped onion
1/2 cup chopped celery
1 clove of garlic, minced or 1/4 tsp. garlic powder
6 green olives, chopped
1 16-oz. can tomatoes
1 cup tomato sauce
1/2 cup chopped green pepper
1/2 cup chopped sweet red pepper
1 bay leaf
A pinch of thyme
1/2 tsp. ground cumin
1/8 tsp. cayenne pepper
1 tsp. chopped fresh parsley
1/4 tsp. sea salt
2 Tbsp. apple juice concentrate
1 lb. tofu, cut into bite-sized pieces
1/4 cup HOT TACO SAUCE p. 189 (more to taste)

In a large saucepan, melt the butter and sauté the onions, garlic, celery and olives, until the onions are transparent. Add the remaining ingredients and simmer, uncovered, for about 45 minutes. (If the sauce needs thickening, dissolve 2 Tbsp. potato starch, cornstarch or arrowroot in a little cold water and add to the mixture; stir continuously until thickened.) Serve in the center of a rice ring and garnish with a little fresh parsley. Serves 4.

TOFU CROQUETTES

3 cups cooked BROWN RICE p. 132
2 lb. tofu, crumbled
1/2 cup rice flour
2 Tbsp. butter or soy margarine
1 cup chopped celery
1/2 cup chopped onion
1/4 cup chopped fresh parsley
1/4 cup tamari
3 eggs or equivalent egg replacer
2 tsp. powdered vegetable broth
1-2 tsp. herb seasoning salt or sea salt
1/4 tsp. garlic powder
1 8-oz. can water chestnuts, chopped
1/2 cup PEANUT BUTTER p. 10
1/2 cup chopped walnuts
Enough gravy to moisten
Buttermilk, optional

In a large mixing bowl, combine the rice, tofu, and flour and set aside. Sauté the celery and onions in the butter until tender. Add the remaining ingredients and mix well. Combine with the rice-tofu mixture and work with your hands until well mixed. Form into patties or cone-shaped croquettes and place on an oiled baking sheet; coat the tops with buttermilk and bake in a preheated oven at 375°F. for about 30 minutes. Serve with gravy. Makes about 2 dozen patties.

TOFU EGG(LESS) SALAD I

1 lb. tofu
3 Tbsp. Dijon-style mustard
1-2 tsp. curry powder
1 tsp. dried or 2 tsp. fresh basil
1/3 cup TOFU MAYONNAISE p. 147
2-3 green onions, chopped
2-3 stalks celery, chopped
1/4 cup chopped fresh parsley
1 tsp. herb seasoning salt or 1/2 tsp. sea salt
Freshly ground pepper to taste

In a large bowl, crumble the tofu; add the remaining ingredients and mix well. Serve as a tomato stuffing, a dip for crackers or in a pita bread sandwich with lettuce and tomato. Serves 4.

TOFU EGG(LESS) SALAD II

1 lb. tofu
3 Tbsp. Dijon-style mustard
3 Tbsp. diced sweet red pepper
8-10 green olives, chopped
1/3 cup TOFU MAYONNAISE p. 147
2 green onions, chopped
2-3 stalks celery, chopped
1 tsp. herb seasoning salt or 1/2 tsp. salt
Freshly ground pepper to taste

Crumble the tofu; add the remaining ingredients and mix well. Serve as a tomato stuffing, a dip for crackers or in pita bread with lettuce and tomato. Serves 4.

TOFU EGG(LESS) SALAD III

1 lb. tofu, crumbled
1/4 cup TOFU MAYONNAISE p. 147
1 Tbsp. each tamari and Dijon-style mustard
1/8 tsp. each ground cumin and tumeric
1/4 tsp. paprika
1 green onion, minced
1/4 cup each chopped celery and green pepper
1/4 cup grated carrot

Combine all the ingredients and mix well. Serve as a stuffing for fresh tomatoes or green peppers or top with alfalfa sprouts in a sandwich. Makes about 3 cups.

TOFU FRITTERS

2 lb. tofu
1 medium onion, chopped
1 large red or green pepper, chopped
1/2 cup chopped fresh parsley
2 tsp. ground cumin
1 tsp. sea salt
1 cup HOT TACO SAUCE p. 189
4 cilantro (fresh coriander) leaves, chopped
2 eggs or equivalent egg replacer
1 1/2 cups brown rice flour

Heat oil in a deep-fryer. Crumble the tofu in a large mixing bowl; mix in the remaining ingredients. Drop by the tablespoonful into the hot oil; fry until golden brown. Serve with HOT TACO SAUCE, rice and vegetables. Makes about 2 dozen fritters.

TOFU KEBABS

2 large green peppers (cut into 8 pieces each)
2 large tomatoes (cut into 8 pieces each)
16 chunks fresh pineapple
16 large mushrooms
16 small white onions
2 lb. tofu (cut into 16 cubes each)
1 1/2 cups CREAMY GARLIC DRESSING p. 166
1 12-oz. can tomato purée
Tamari and freshly ground pepper to taste

Preheat the oven to 450°F. Using 16 Chinese wooden skewers, alternate 1 each of the vegetables and pineapple pieces and 2 tofu cubes per skewer. Place the skewers in a large, oiled baking pan. (Any extra vegetables can be placed in the bottom of the pan.) Sprinkle with tamari and pepper. Mix the dressing and tomato purée together well and pour over the skewers. Bake covered for 30 minutes, basting occasionally. Remove the cover when the vegetables are tender; bake uncovered at 500°F. until the vegetables have a charred look, about 20 minutes. Remove from the oven and serve 2 skewers per person with rice. Serves 8.

TOFU-MUSHROOM STROGANOFF

2 lb. tofu
Vegetable oil
1 lb. fresh mushrooms
1 Tbsp. butter or soy margarine
1 Tbsp. wine of choice

Continued next page...

1/2 cup tamari
1/2 tsp. garlic powder
2 tsp. dried chives
1/4 cup wine of choice
1 tsp. powdered vegetable broth
1/2 cup water
Several good turns freshly ground pepper
1 medium onion, thinly sliced
1/2 cup tomato purée
2 Tbsp. ROUX p. 147
1 cup sour cream
1 pkg. Jerusalem artichoke or rice noodles

Slice the tofu into thin strips (about 1/4-inch thick, 3/4-inch wide and 3 inches long). Heat the oil in a large skillet and fry the tofu strips on both sides until golden brown and crisp. (Use 2 skillets to save time.) Drain on paper towels and set aside.

Wipe the mushrooms clean with a damp cloth (don't soak as they absorb too much water); slice in half. Melt the butter in a skillet; add 1 Tbsp. of wine and the mushrooms. Cover and sauté for about 5 minutes on medium-high heat. Remove from the heat, strain and reserve the liquid for later. (Start the noodles cooking.)

Meanwhile, mix the tamari, garlic powder, chives, wine, powdered broth, water, pepper and onions in a saucepan; bring to a boil. Reduce the heat and simmer until tender, about 5 minutes. Add the tomato purée and mushroom liquid; whisk in the ROUX to thicken. Add the mushrooms and tofu; simmer to blend the flavors, about 5 minutes. Remove from the heat; add the sour cream and serve over a bed of hot noodles. Serves 6.

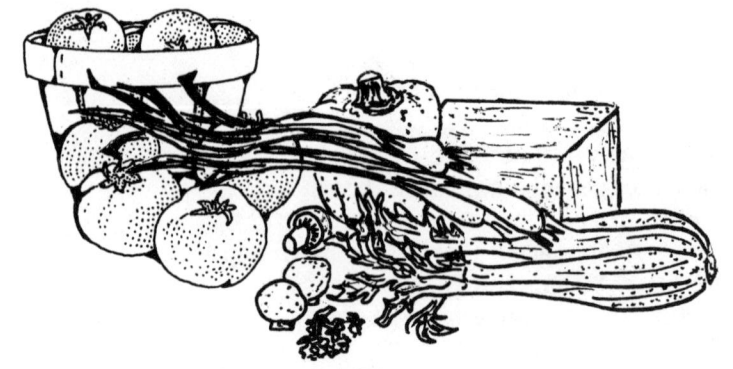

TOFU ROAST

2 lb. tofu
1 large onion, chopped
2-3 stalks celery, chopped
1/2 lb. mushrooms, chopped
1 cup chopped red and/or green pepper
1/2 cup tomato purée
2 tsp. powdered vegetable broth
Tamari
1-2 tsp. poultry seasoning
Sea salt or herb seasoning salt and pepper to taste

Preheat the oven to 350°F. In a large mixing bowl, crumble the tofu and set aside. Sauté the vegetables in a little oil; stir in the tomato purée, powdered broth and seasonings. Add to the crumbled tofu and mix. Form into a loaf in an oiled loaf pan; bake until solid but not dry, about 1 hour. Makes 1 loaf.

VARIATION:
In an oiled oven-proof bowl, form the mix into a crust 1-inch thick and bake until firm. When cool, stuff with B R'S ENDIVE POTATOES p. 218 and return to the oven to warm. To serve, invert on a platter so that the TOFU ROAST is on top, then slice. Serves 6.

TOFU SLOPPY JOES

1 clove garlic, minced
3 small green peppers, chopped
1 large onion, chopped
3 Tbsp. oil
1 lb. tofu, crumbled
1 1/2 cups thick tomato sauce
3 heaping Tbsp. Dijon-style mustard
1 tsp. chili powder
Italian herbs, sea salt and pepper to taste

Sauté the garlic, green peppers and onion in the oil until tender; add the remaining ingredients; mix well and simmer until the sauce cooks down. Adjust the seasoning and serve over brown rice or on fresh buns with lettuce, sliced onion and sprouts. Serves 4-6.

TOFU STEAK

Leftover MUSHROOM-BARLEY SOUP p. 207
6 thin slices tofu, per person
1 sliced green onion, per person
2 slices whole-grain toast, per person

Purée the leftover soup into a thick gravy and set aside. Fry the tofu until golden brown on both sides. (Or bake at 400°F. for 20 minutes on each side.) Sauté the green onions until tender; add the tofu and soup gravy (add a little water if needed to thin). Simmer about 15 minutes to blend the flavors and serve over buttered toast as an open-faced sandwich, with a tomato salad and homemade french fries.

TOFU TETRAZZINI

2 lb. tofu
8 oz. macaroni (Jerusalem artichoke or whole wheat)
1/2 cup chopped onion
1 lb. mushrooms
1 whole clove garlic, peeled
5 Tbsp. butter or soy margarine
1/2 cup blanched, slivered almonds
5-6 Tbsp. flour
2 cups vegetable stock
1/2 tsp. ground white pepper and sea salt to taste
1/4 tsp. each ground coriander and cayenne pepper
1 cup heated dairy or CASHEW CREAM p. 182
1/4 cup each dry white wine and liquid soy protein
2 Tbsp. white miso
Grated Parmesan cheese, optional

Drop the tofu into boiling water for 3-4 minutes to freshen; cut into julienne-style strips and set aside. Cook the macaroni (slightly underdone) and set aside. Wipe the mushrooms clean, slice in half and sauté with the onions and garlic clove in 2 Tbsp. of the butter. Discard the garlic and toss with the macaroni. Add the slivered almonds and season to taste; set aside.

In a saucepan, melt the remaining 3 Tbsp. butter; stir in the flour to form a paste and slowly add the vegetable broth, stirring continuously until thickened. Remove from the heat; season to taste. Stir in the miso, mixed with the cream; add the wine and set aside.

Preheat the oven to 375°F. Combine the tofu, macaroni mixture and sauce in a large, oiled casserole dish. Top with Parmesan cheese and bake for 20-30 minutes. Serve with a colorful salad. Serves 6-8.

TOFU TURKEY

2 cups oatmeal
2 cups hot water
1 cup finely chopped mushrooms
1 medium onion, finely chopped
1 cup finely chopped celery
1 cup chopped pecans (or walnuts)
1 lb. tofu, crumbled
2 Tbsp. oil
2 Tbsp. PEANUT BUTTER p. 10
2 Tbsp. tamari
2 tsp. poultry seasoning (or 1/2 tsp. each sage and paprika and 1/4 tsp. each basil, marjoram, thyme and rosemary)
1/2-1 tsp. sea salt
Freshly ground black pepper to taste
BROWN RICE STUFFING p. 133

Pour the hot water over the oatmeal and mix well. Add the remaining ingredients; blend together well. Butter a stainless steel or oven-proof bowl and press the mixture into a thick crust around the inside of the bowl. Bake at 350°F. for about 45 minutes, until browned and firm to the touch. Fill the crust with the BROWN RICE STUFFING. Invert the bowl on a platter and garnish the stuffed "turkey" with tomato slices and parsley sprigs. Serves 8.

VARIATION:
Butter the bottom and side of a loaf pan and add the tofu mixture. Bake at 350°F. for at least 1 hour. Invert the loaf on a platter and surround with stuffing; garnish the loaf with tomato slices and parsley sprigs.

TOFU-VEGETABLE STEW

1/4 cup oil
1 cup each sliced onion, carrot, and celery
1 clove garlic, minced
1 lb. tofu, cut into bite-sized pieces
1/4 tamari
1 1/2 cups sliced yellow squash
1 cup shredded cabbage
2 tomatoes, diced
1 1/2 tsp. dried or 1 Tbsp. chopped fresh basil
1/4 tsp. summer savory and 1 bay leaf
2 cups tomato juice

In a large soup pot, sauté the onions, carrots, celery and garlic in the oil until tender. Marinate the tofu in the tamari; stir into the pot with the remaining ingredients. Simmer for 1 hour and serve with brown rice and a green salad. Serves 6-8.

TOFU WITH WALNUTS

1/4 cup tamari or 1/3 cup liquid soy protein
2 tsp. cornstarch, potato starch or arrowroot
1/4 cup sherry or dry wine
1 tsp. grated ginger and 1/2 tsp. cayenne pepper
1 Tbsp. apple juice concentrate
1 lb. tofu, cut into bite-sized pieces
2 Tbsp. oil
2 medium green peppers, cut into 1/2-inch pieces
4 green onions, bias-sliced into 1-inch lengths
1 cup walnut halves

Continued next page...

In a small bowl, combine the tamari, starch or arrowroot, sherry, ginger, apple concentrate, and cayenne. Pour over the tofu; set aside to marinate. Preheat a wok or large skillet; add the oil and stir-fry the peppers and onions until tender-crisp. Remove from the wok. Stir-fry the walnuts for 2 minutes and remove. Add more oil, if necessary; stir-fry the tofu and marinade for 5 minutes, stirring until thickened. Mix in the vegetables and walnuts; cover and cook 1 more minute. Serve over brown rice. Serves 4-6.

VEGETABLE ENCHILADAS

1 medium onion, chopped
1 sweet red pepper, chopped
1 green bell pepper, chopped
3 cups fresh corn kernels or 2 pkg. frozen corn
1 cup HOT TACO SAUCE p. 189
4 cups cooked kidney or pinto beans, drained
12 corn tortillas
MEXICAN TOMATO SAUCE p. 191
Grated cheese or TOFU "RICOTTA CHEESE" p. 148

Sauté the onion and peppers in a large skillet until tender. (Set aside 1/2 cup of the mixture to use in the sauce.) Add the corn and hot sauce and simmer. Meanwhile, purée the beans in a food processor; turn into a skillet and refry until thickened. Quick-fry the corn tortillas until soft and flexible; drain on paper towels. Spoon some beans and vegetable mix into the center of each tortilla, top with the cheese and roll. Place the rolls, seam down, in a large casserole dish. Prepare the MEXICAN TOMATO SAUCE and pour over the enchiladas; top with cheese. Bake at 350°F. for 30 minutes and serve with rice. Serves 6.

VEGETABLE-STUFFED TOFU

Oil for deep-frying
2 lb. tofu
1/2 lb. mushrooms, finely chopped
6 green onions, finely chopped
1 cup finely chopped bean sprouts
Tamari to taste
1 tsp. sesame oil (toasted, if available)
Rice flour

Heat a deep-fryer or a skillet filled with 2 inches of oil. Cut the tofu into 4 pieces by cutting the block diagonally to form 2 triangles and then cutting each triangle in half, forming 4. Repeat for the second pound so that 8 triangles are ready for use. Then scoop out a pocket on the longest side of each triangle. Each tofu shell should be about 1/2-inch thick on all sides. (Save the scoops for another recipe such as TOFU EGG(LESS) SALAD p. 118 or TOFU MAYONNAISE p. 147.)

Finely chop the mushrooms, green onions and bean sprouts. In a large skillet, sauté the mushrooms and green onions well before adding the bean sprouts as they only take about 1 minute to cook. Add the tamari and the sesame oil; stir and set aside.

Coat the tofu triangles in the rice flour and sprinkle with salt and pepper. When the oil is hot, drop them in the deep-fryer and fry until golden brown. Drain on paper towels. Stuff the tofu triangles with the sautéed vegetables and serve with SWEET AND SPICY MISO GRAVY p. 194 and rice. Serves 4.

Grain Side Dishes

About Grains, 130
Barley-Mushroom Bake, 132
Brown Rice, 132
Brown Rice and Corn, 133
Brown Rice Stuffing, 134
Bulgur Casserole, 134
Bulgur-Rice, 135
Homestyle Kasha, 136
Macaroni Garden Salad, 137
Millet, 137
Mushroom-Rice Ring, 138
Nut-Fruit Tabouli, 138
Rice-Vegetable Salad, 139
Rice-Walnut Salad, 140
Tabouli, 140
Tomato Rice, 141
Wild Rice-Artichoke Casserole, 142

GRAIN COOKING TIME

One cup of grain (unsoaked)	Amount of water	Regular cooking time	Pressure cooker time
Rolled, flaked or cracked grain (oatmeal, cracked wheat, rye, etc.)	2 cups	5–10 min.	—
Cracked, parboiled or soft grains (bulgur, buckwheat, cracked wheat, kasha, millet)	2½ cups	20 min.	10 min.
Medium whole grains (hulled barley, brown rice)	2 cups	40–55 min.	30 min.
Hard whole grains (oats, rye, triticale, wheat berries)	2½ cups	1–1½ hrs.	45 min.

NOTES:
1. Rolled flakes or cracked grains are *not recommended for pressure-cooking* because of their tendency to clog the steam vent.
2. The amount of water and length of cooking time will vary, depending on the source of heat and type of cooking pot used; adjust accordingly.
3. For pressure cooking: The amount of water used may be reduced slightly when cooking more than one cup of a grain – but there is no specific ratio. Experiment with the different grains in your specific situation.

ABOUT GRAINS

This section includes a few suggested side dishes using whole or slightly processed grains. Because grains are the mainstay of a vegetarian diet, more grain recipes are spread throughout the other sections of this book or are suggested accompaniments to many non-grain recipes. (Also see individual grains in the Glossary and Index.)

The less processing done to a grain, the greater its nutritional value. Therefore, whenever possible, use whole grains, and whenever practical, grind them to make your own cereals and flours. Combining whole grains and legumes (beans, peas, lentils) in a 2:1 ratio produces complete, balanced, usable proteins. In addition to providing extra nutritional value, flavor and texture to your meals, whole grains are relatively inexpensive and can be prepared in time- and energy-conserving ways. See the following cooking methods:

PRESOAKING: Presoaking the hard grains (whole wheat berries, hulled rye, oats, etc.) overnight or bringing to a boil then soaking for 2 hours, will reduce the cooking time by about 1/3.

REGULAR COOKING: Wash the grains well in cold water. Place the water (refer to the GRAIN COOKING TIMES chart for the appropriate amount) in a heavy pot with tight-fitting lid; add salt, if desired, and bring to a boil. Stir in the grain and return to a boil. Cover, reduce the heat and simmer for the time suggested on the chart. (DO NOT stir again until ready to serve or the grains will become sticky.) When the

Continued next page...

cooking time is up, turn off the heat and leave the pot on the cooking burner until ready to serve.

PRESSURE COOKING: Follow the same procedures as for REGULAR COOKING up through the point of covering the pot. Then bring the pressure up to 15 lbs. and cook for the suggested time (see chart). When the cooking time is up, cool immediately under water to release the pressure; cover again and set aside, away from the heat, until ready to serve.

OR: Place 1 or 2 inches of water in the bottom of the pressure cooker. Place the measured grain in a stainless steel bowl inside the cooker and add water to fill the bowl about 3/4 to 1 inch above the grain. Cover, then continue the pressure-cooking process. (This is a good way to cook beans and grains at the same time — beans on the bottom, grains in the bowl, on top.)

THERMOS COOKING: <u>For rolled or cracked grains</u> — preheat a wide-mouth thermos bottle (fill it with hot water and empty just before using). Fill the preheated thermos 1/4 full with any rolled or cracked grain. Then pour in boiling water 3/4 full; close tightly and lay the thermos on its side for 8-10 hours. Open when ready to serve.

<u>For whole grains</u> — Measure enough of the desired whole grain to fill 1/4 of a wide-mouth thermos bottle, then presoak (see chart p. 129). Measure enough water to fill the thermos 1/2 full and place in a saucepan with the presoaked grain; bring to a boil and pour into the preheated thermos (it should be 3/4 full). Close tightly and lay the thermos on its side for 8-10 hours. Open when ready to serve.

BARLEY-MUSHROOM BAKE

1/4 cup oil
1/2 cup chopped green onions
1/2 cup chopped carrot
1/2 lb. mushrooms, sliced
1 cup barley, washed
1 tsp. powdered vegetable broth
2 1/2 cups vegetable stock or water
1/8 tsp. marjoram
Sea salt and pepper to taste

Preheat the oven to 350°F; in a large skillet, sauté the vegetables and barley in the oil until lightly browned. Dissolve the powdered broth in the vegetable stock and bring to a boil. Add the barley mixture and seasonings and pour into a large casserole dish; cover and bake for 1 hour. Serves 4.

BROWN RICE

2 cups brown rice
4 cups water

Rinse the brown rice well; drain and set aside. Bring the water to a boil in a large saucepan. Add the rice, stir once (do not stir again or it will become sticky). Cover, reduce the heat and simmer for 55 minutes (until the water is absorbed). Turn off the heat and let the cooked rice sit on the warm burner until ready to serve. Makes about 5 cups.

Continued next page...

VARIATIONS:
1. Substitute tomato juice, fruit juice or vegetable bouillon for the water.
2. Top hot cooked rice with butter and chopped parsley, chives or celery seeds.
3. Add 1/2 cup washed millet or kasha and 1 more cup water to the rice and cook together.

BROWN RICE AND CORN

1/3 cup dried whole corn kernels
1 1/2 cups brown rice
3 cups water
1/2 cup chopped sweet red peppers
1/2 cup chopped onions
2 Tbsp. oil or butter
1/4 cup chopped fresh parsley
Sea salt and pepper to taste

Soak the corn kernels in water overnight; drain. Wash the rice and drain. Bring the water to a boil and add the corn and rice; cover and simmer for 1 hour. Sauté the peppers and onions in the oil; toss with the parsley into the cooked grains. Season to taste and serve. Serves 8.

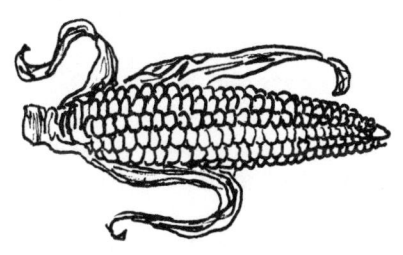

BROWN RICE STUFFING

2 cups cooked BROWN RICE p. 132
1 cup fresh or frozen green peas
1 large carrot, finely chopped
1 cup pecans, finely chopped
1/4 cup butter or soy margarine
Sea salt or herb seasoning salt and pepper to taste

Cook the BROWN RICE as directed in the recipe; turn off the heat and leave on the burner. Steam the carrots for about 5 minutes; add the peas and steam a few more minutes until the vegetables are tender. Add the steamed vegetables, pecans, butter and seasonings to the cooked rice and mix well. Use as a stuffing for the TOFU TURKEY mold p. 125 or serve as a side dish. Makes about 6 cups.

BULGUR CASSEROLE

2 Tbsp. oil
1/2 cup chopped green onions
2 cups cooked corn kernels
2 cups cooked carrots, cut julienne-style
1/2 tsp. marjoram
3 Tbsp. chopped fresh parsley
1 Tbsp. powdered vegetable broth
4 cups vegetable stock or water
1 1/2 cups bulgur (see Glossary — Grains)
Sea salt and pepper to taste

Continued next page...

In a large skillet, sauté the onions in the oil until tender. Stir in the corn, carrots, and herbs; simmer for 5 minutes. In a large casserole dish, dissolve the powdered broth in the water and add the bulgur. Stir in the sautéed vegetables and adjust the seasoning. Cover and bake for 20 minutes at 350°F. Serves 8.

BULGUR-RICE

1/2 cup bulgur (see Glossary — Grains)
1 cup brown rice
3 cups water

Rinse the bulgur and rice well; drain and set aside. Bring the water to a boil in a large saucepan. Add the bulgur and rice, stir once (do not stir again or it will become sticky). Cover, reduce the heat and simmer for 55 minutes (until the water is absorbed). Turn off the heat and let the cooked grains sit on the warm burner until ready to serve. Serve with GRAVY I or II p. 188 and beans. Makes 4 cups.

VARIATIONS:
1. Substitute tomato juice, fruit juice or vegetable bouillon for the water.
2. Top hot cooked grains with butter and chopped parsley, chives or celery seeds.
3. Add nuts and seeds to the cooked grains before serving.

HOMESTYLE KASHA

2 1/2 cups water
1/2 tsp. sea salt
1 1/2 cups diced potatoes
1 cup whole groats or coarse kasha (roasted buckwheat)
1/4 cup butter or soy margarine
1 small onion, chopped
1/4 cup chopped green pepper
1/4 cup chopped sweet red pepper
1/8 tsp. garlic powder
1 tsp. summer savory
Paprika
Yogurt, optional

Place the water, salt, and potatoes in a saucepan; bring to a boil and cook for 5 minutes. Add the kasha; reduce the heat and simmer for 10-15 minutes until the water is absorbed. In a large skillet, sauté the onions and green pepper in the butter until tender. Stir in the garlic powder, savory and kasha mixture; fry like hash browns for 20-30 minutes. Sprinkle with paprika and serve with yogurt, if desired. Serves 4-6.

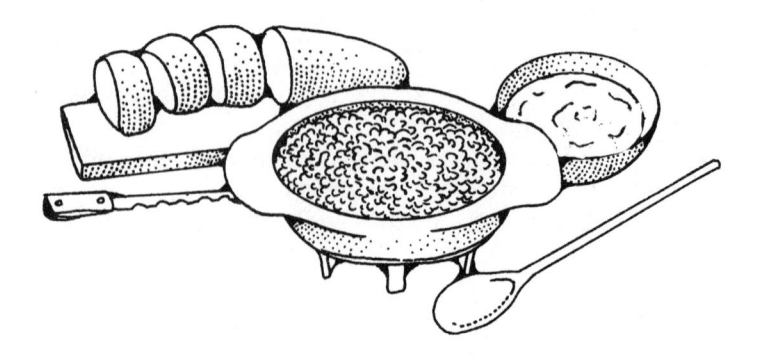

MACARONI GARDEN SALAD

1 12-oz. pkg. macaroni (Jerusalem artichoke or whole wheat)
1 cup each chopped cucumber and sliced celery
1/2 cup diced green pepper
1/4 cup diced sweet red pepper
1 small red onion, thinly sliced
1/4 cup chopped parsley or watercress
1 cup cooked green beans, cut in 1-inch pieces
1/4 cup sliced ripe olives
1 tsp. dried or 2 tsp. minced fresh basil
1 cup TOFU MAYONNAISE p. 147 or MISO DRESSING II p. 171
Sea salt or herb seasoning salt and pepper to taste

Cook the macaroni as directed. Combine all the ingredients in a large mixing bowl; toss gently until well coated with the mayonnaise and chill. Serves 8.

MILLET

1 1/2 cups millet
3 cups water
1 tsp. powdered vegetable broth, optional

Wash the millet well; drain and set aside. Bring the water to a boil; add the millet and powdered broth, stir once and cover. (Do not stir while cooking or it will become sticky.) Simmer until the water is absorbed, about 20 minutes. Serve plain with butter or gravy, or mixed with sautéed green onions, parsley and red or green peppers. Makes about 3 1/2 cups.

MUSHROOM-RICE RING

1/4 cup chopped onion
1/2 lb. mushrooms, chopped
Squeeze of lemon, optional
2 Tbsp. butter or soy margarine
1 cup cooked BROWN RICE p. 132
1/2 cup slivered, blanched almonds, roasted
Sea salt and pepper to taste

Sauté the mushrooms and onions in the butter and lemon juice; add the remaining ingredients, adjust the seasoning and heat thoroughly. Press the mixture firmly into a buttered ring mold and let stand for about 5 minutes. Invert the rice mold on a platter and fill the center with buttered, steamed vegetables. Serves 4.

NUT-FRUIT TABOULI

1 cup bulgur (see Glossary — Grains)
1/4 tsp. each ground cinnamon, nutmeg and cloves
Apple juice to cover
1/4 cup each chopped almonds, peanuts, cashews and walnuts
2 Tbsp. GOMASIO p. 144 (ground toasted sesame seeds)
1/4 cup pumpkin seeds
1/4 cup each raisins and chopped dates
2 Tbsp. lemon juice, optional
2 Tbsp. oil, optional
1/8 tsp. sea salt, optional
1/4 tsp. cayenne pepper, optional

Continued next page...

Place the bulgur and spices in a large bowl; pour in heated apple juice to just cover the grain. Cover and set aside for about 30 minutes until the juice is completely absorbed. Add the remaining ingredients; toss and chill for several hours before serving as a breakfast cereal, a salad or a side dish. Serves 4-6.

RICE-VEGETABLE SALAD

2 cups cooked BROWN RICE p. 132
1/2 cup diced celery
1/2 cup diced red and/or green pepper
1/2 cup sliced green onions
2 tomatoes, diced
3 Tbsp. chopped fresh parsley
3 Tbsp. chopped watercress
1/2 tsp. chopped fresh basil
MISO DRESSING II p. 171
Sea salt or herb seasoning salt and pepper to taste

Combine the rice, vegetables and herbs; mix well. Pour the dressing over the rice mixture and toss. Adjust the seasoning to taste; cover and refrigerate for several hours before serving. Garnish with fresh parsley and tomato wedges. Serves 6-8.

RICE-WALNUT SALAD

2 1/2 cups cooked BROWN RICE p. 132
1/2 cup chopped green onions
1/2 cup diced cucumber
1/2 large carrot, grated
1/2 cup chopped fresh parsley
3/4 cup coarsely chopped walnuts
1 apple, grated
CREAMY CURRY DRESSING p. 166
Sea salt and pepper to taste

Combine the rice, onion, cucumber, carrot, parsley and walnuts; chill well. Grate the apple into the dressing and toss with the salad. Season to taste and arrange on a plate of lettuce leaves; garnish with tomato wedges. Serves 8.

TABOULI

1 cup bulgur (see Glossary — Grains)
Boiling water or vegetable stock to cover
1/2 cup sliced green onions with tops
1/2 cup chopped fresh parsley
2 Tbsp. dried or 3 Tbsp. fresh mint
2/3 cup chopped toasted almonds
1/2 cup chopped sweet red pepper
1/2 cup diced tomatoes
1/4 cup diced cucumber
3/4-1 cup MISO DRESSING II p. 171

Continued next page...

Place the bulgur in a large bowl; pour in boiling water or vegetable stock to just cover the grain. Cover and set aside for about 30 minutes until the water is completely absorbed. Add the remaining ingredients; toss and chill for several hours before serving as a side dish or as a salad on lettuce leaves. Serves 6-8.

TOMATO RICE

3 Tbsp. oil
1 1/2 cups brown rice, washed and drained
1 large onion, chopped
2 cloves garlic, minced
1/2 tsp. ginger
1/2 tsp. ground coriander
1/4 tsp. ground cloves
1/8 tsp. freshly ground black pepper
1 tsp. sea salt
3 cups tomatoes, puréed
1/2 cup cooked green peas for garnish

Set the peas aside. In a large saucepan, heat the oil and stir in the rice; sauté for about 5 minutes, stirring frequently until the rice is browned and well coated with oil. Add the onion and garlic and sauté until golden brown. In a separate pan, combine the seasonings and tomatoes; bring to a boil. Then stir into the rice (do not stir again or it will become sticky); cover and simmer on medium-low heat for about 50-55 minutes, until all of the liquid has been absorbed. Allow to sit on the cooling burner for at least 15 minutes. Add the peas, adjust the seasoning and toss before serving. Serves 8.

WILD RICE-ARTICHOKE CASSEROLE

3 cups cooked artichoke hearts (fresh or frozen)
1 1/2 cups cooked BROWN RICE p. 132
1 1/2 cups cooked wild rice
1 Tbsp. powdered vegetable broth
1 cup boiling vegetable stock or water
1 tsp. thyme
1/4 cup butter or soy margarine

Slice the artichoke hearts in half and combine with the rice in a large casserole dish. Dissolve the powdered broth in the water; add the thyme and pour over the rice mixture. Bake for 30 minutes at 325°F. Dot with the butter and bake 10 minutes more. Serves 4-6.

Miscellaneous

Gomasio, 144
Herb Croutons, 144
Low-Fat "Cream Cheese," 145
Low-Fat "Sour Cream," 145
Mock "Cream Cheese," 146
Mock "Sour Cream," 146
Roux, 147
Tofu Mayonnaise, 147
Tofu "Ricotta Cheese," 148

GOMASIO

Roast sesame seeds in a non-stick skillet on medium-low heat, stirring continuously. When the seeds are golden brown, remove from the pan; cool and grind in a food processor or blender to a fine consistency. Add sea salt or use plain. Use to flavor soups and salads.

HERB CROUTONS

Cut bread slices into 1/2-inch cubes. Melt butter in a skillet and add the bread cubes. Toss the cubes continuously until all sides are browned and crisp; add chopped parsley, garlic powder, Parmesan cheese or any herbs that complement the soup or salad with which they will be served.

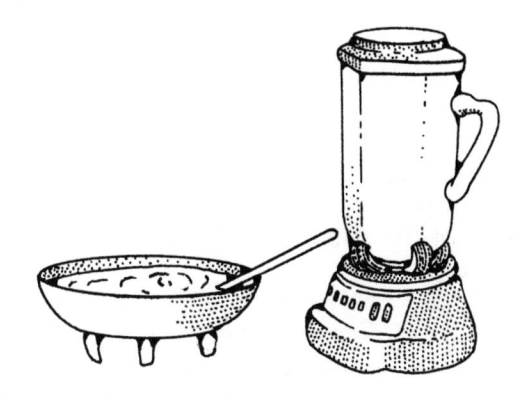

LOW-FAT "CREAM CHEESE"

1 1/2 cups low-fat cottage cheese
1/4 cup buttermilk or yogurt
1/4 cup skim milk
1 Tbsp. instant non-fat dry milk

In a blender or food processor, combine all the ingredients and blend until very smooth. Cover and refrigerate until thickened into a cream cheese consistency. Makes 2 cups.

LOW-FAT "SOUR CREAM"

1/2 cup skim milk
1/2 cup farmer's, ricotta or low-fat cottage cheese

In a blender or food processor, blend the cheese and milk to the desired consistency. Serve whenever sour cream would be appropriate. Makes 1 cup.

MOCK "CREAM CHEESE"

2 tsp. agar-agar flakes
2 Tbsp. water
2 Tbsp. white miso
1/8 lb. tofu
2 Tbsp. oil
1 Tbsp. fresh lemon juice
1/4 tsp. vanilla extract
1 tsp. maple syrup or apple juice concentrate

Heat the agar-agar and water in a small saucepan, stirring continuously; blend with the remaining ingredients in a food processor or blender until smooth. Chill well; serve in place of dairy cream cheese. Makes about 3/4 cup.

MOCK "SOUR CREAM"

1/2 cup NUT MILK p. 23
1/4 lb. TOFU "RICOTTA CHEESE" p. 148

Blend the ingredients together well; chill and serve in place of dairy sour cream. Makes about 3/4 cup.

ROUX

1/2 cup unsalted butter
1 Tbsp. oil
1 cup flour (unbleached, whole wheat, rice flour, etc.)

Melt the butter in a small saucepan; add the oil and stir in the flour. Cook for 3 minutes, stirring continuously, until thickened. Can be kept refrigerated in a covered container for a couple of months. Use in TOFU-MUSHROOM STROGANOFF p. 120 or as needed to thicken soups and sauces. Makes 1 1/2 cups.

TOFU MAYONNAISE

1 lb. tofu
1/3 cup oil
1/3 cup lemon juice
1/2 tsp. onion powder
1/2 tsp. dry mustard
1 tsp. herb seasoning salt or 1/2 tsp. sea salt
1/8 tsp. garlic powder or to taste
1 tsp. apple juice concentrate
(Italian herbs to taste for variety)

Blend the tofu in a food processor until smooth; add the oil, lemon juice and seasonings and blend. Add more oil or lemon juice or a little water to adjust the consistency. Makes about 2 1/2 cups.

TOFU "RICOTTA CHEESE"

1 lb. tofu
2 Tbsp. oil
1/4 cup lemon juice
1/4 tsp. basil
1 tsp. Italian herbs
1/8 tsp. garlic powder or 1 small clove garlic
3 green onions, chopped or 1/4 tsp. onion powder
2 tsp. chopped fresh or 1 tsp. dried parsley
1 tsp. powdered vegetable broth
1/2 tsp. sea salt or to taste

Blend the tofu and oil in a food processor until creamy. Add the lemon juice, herbs, green onions and salt; mix well. Use in LASAGNA p. 98, manicotti, etc. Makes about 2 1/2 cups.

Salads and Salad Dressings

SALADS

Apple-Tangerine Salad, 150
Avocado Salad, 150
Black-Eyed Pea Salad, 151
Blended Salad, 151
Broccoli-Cauliflower Salad, 152
Carrot-Raisin Salad, 152
Coleslaw, 153
Confetti Bean Salad, 153
Cooked Vegetable Salads, 154
Cucumber Mousse, 155
Fresh Corn Salad, 156
Fresh Fruit Cup, 156
Green Bean Aspic, 157
Jerusalem Artichoke Salad, 158
Middle Eastern Slaw, 158
Potato-Pecan Salad, 159
Potato-Vegetable Salad, 159
Stuffed Beets, 160
Summer Garden Salad, 161
Tangy Apple Mold, 161
Tomatoes with Basil, 162
Tropical Waldorf Salad, 162
Vegetable Aspic, 163
Watercress and Green Bean Salad, 164
Watercress-Sprout Salad, 164

SALAD DRESSINGS

Avocado Dressing, 165
Coleslaw Dressing, 165
Creamy Curry Dressing, 166
Creamy Garlic Dressing, 166
Cucumber Dressing, 167
Curried Fruit Dressing, 167
Curried Tomato Dressing, 168
Easy Sesame Dressing, 168
French Lemon Dressing, 169
Green Goddess Dressing, 169
Herb Dressing, 170
Italian Dressing, 170
Miso Dressing I, 171
Miso Dressing II, 171
Mustard Dressing, 172
"Sour Cream" Dressing, 172

SALADS

APPLE-TANGERINE SALAD

1 red Delicious apple and lemon juice
1/2 cup walnut pieces
1 Tbsp. butter or soy margarine
1/4 tsp. garlic powder
Romaine lettuce
1/2 cup golden raisins
1 fresh tangerine, peeled and sectioned
Oil and lemon juice
Oregano or mixed Italian herbs
Sea salt and pepper to taste

Core and dice the apple; coat lightly with lemon juice and set aside. Sauté the walnut pieces in the butter and garlic; set aside to cool. Tear the lettuce into bite-sized pieces and place in a large salad bowl; add the diced apple, tangerines, raisins and walnuts. Sprinkle with oil and lemon juice; season to taste. Toss lightly and serve. Serves 4.

AVOCADO SALAD

2 large avocados, peeled and sliced
2 large tomatoes, wedged
Romaine lettuce and 4 green onions, sliced

Arrange the sliced avocados and tomato wedges on a bed of lettuce; sprinkle with the chopped green onions and ITALIAN, HERB or MISO DRESSING p. 170-1. Serves 6-8.

BLACK-EYED PEA SALAD

1/2 cup chopped celery
1/2 cup chopped green pepper
1/2 cup sliced green onions
1 medium-sized hot pepper, chopped
4 cups cooked black-eyed peas
1 large tomato, coarsely chopped
ITALIAN DRESSING p. 170

In a large bowl, combine all the ingredients and mix well. Chill for at least 1 hour (the longer, the better!). Adjust the seasoning and serve on a bed of lettuce with a garnish of fresh parsley. Serves 6-8.

BLENDED SALAD

1 carrot
1 stalk celery
1/2 green or red bell pepper
1/2 cucumber
Small bunch parsley
10 romaine lettuce leaves
1 tomato
Any other favorite vegetables

In a food processor, separately prepare the following: Grate the carrot; chop the firm vegetables together (celery, peppers, cucumber, parsley); chop the lettuce, a few leaves at a time, then the tomato. Toss all the vegetables together. Add your favorite dressing, toss again and top with garbanzo or other beans, nuts, seeds, grated cheese, etc. Serves 4.

BROCCOLI-CAULIFLOWER SALAD

2 cups broccoli flowerettes
2 cups cauliflowerettes
1/2 cup sliced carrots
1/2 cup sliced celery
1/2 cup sliced green onions
1 cup cherry tomatoes
1/4 cup sliced ripe olives

Steam the broccoli, cauliflower and carrots until tender-crisp; set aside to cool. Combine the steamed vegetables with the remaining ingredients and toss with FRENCH LEMON, HERB or MISO DRESSING I or II p. 169-171; marinate in the refrigerator for several hours before serving. Serves 6-8.

CARROT-RAISIN SALAD

4 medium carrots, grated
1/2 cup raisins
1/2 cup shredded unsweetened coconut
2 Tbsp. lemon juice
1/4 cup. TOFU MAYONNAISE p. 147 or COLESLAW DRESSING p. 165
1 tsp. celery seeds, optional
2 Tbsp. apple juice concentrate, optional

Combine all the ingredients in a large bowl and toss well. Chill and serve on a bed of lettuce leaves. Serves 6-8.

COLESLAW

2 cups shredded green cabbage
1 cup shredded red cabbage
1/2 cup crushed pineapple
1/4 cup golden raisins
COLESLAW DRESSING p. 165
1/2 cup roasted peanuts
2 Tbsp. toasted sunflower seeds

Combine the cabbage, pineapple, raisins and dressing in a large bowl and toss well. Chill thoroughly; stir in the peanuts and sunflower seeds just before serving. Serves 6.

CONFETTI BEAN SALAD

1 cup cooked kidney beans
1 cup cooked garbanzo beans
1 cup cooked green beans, cut in 1-inch pieces
1 1/2 cups cooked corn kernels
1/2 cup chopped green pepper
1/2 cup chopped sweet red pepper
1/2 cup sliced celery
1/4 cup sliced green onions
FRENCH LEMON or ITALIAN DRESSING p. 169-170

Combine all the ingredients in a large bowl and toss gently until well coated with the dressing of choice. Cover and refrigerate several hours or overnight. Serve on a bed of lettuce. Serves 6-8.

COOKED VEGETABLE SALADS

The following salad suggestions make use of chilled pre-cooked vegetables, thus providing a tasty way to use leftovers. Combine the ingredients for each salad and toss gently with the suggested dressing or one of your favorite dressings. Experiment with your own leftover combinations. Each combination serves 4-6.

1. 2 cups cooked French green beans
   2 cups steamed celery slices
   4 cups chopped salad greens
   FRENCH LEMON DRESSING p. 169 to taste

2. 2 cups steamed fresh asparagus
   2 cups chopped watercress
   3 cups chopped romaine lettuce
   MUSTARD DRESSING p. 172 to taste

3. 2 cups steamed celery slices
   1/2 lemon, very thinly sliced
   2 cups julienne-cut cooked beets
   3 cups salad greens
   EASY SESAME DRESSING p. 168 to taste

4. 1 cup grated steamed carrots
   1 cup grated steamed beets
   1/2 cup chopped cucumber
   1/2 cup cooked garbanzo beans
   1/2 cup HERB CROUTONS p. 144
   4 cups salad greens
   CUCUMBER DRESSING p. 167 to taste

CUCUMBER MOUSSE

4 Tbsp. agar-agar flakes
1 cup vegetable stock or water
1 cup TOFU MAYONNAISE p. 147
1 Tbsp. sliced green onion
1 Tbsp. lemon juice
1/2 tsp. dried dill
1/4 tsp. sea salt or to taste
1/8 tsp. garlic powder
1/4-1/2 tsp. bottled hot sauce
2 medium cucumbers, peeled
Romaine lettuce
Radish roses and fresh parsley

In a small saucepan, dissolve the agar-agar in the vegetable stock; bring to a boil and simmer for about 5 minutes, stirring continuously. Add the mayonnaise, green onion, lemon juice, dill, salt, garlic and hot sauce. Mix well and set aside to cool. Purée the cucumber in a food processor or blender and add the cooled agar mixture; blend until smooth. Pour into a 5-cup mold or 8 individual molds and chill until firm, about 4 hours or overnight. To serve, unmold onto a lettuce-lined plate; garnish with radish roses and fresh parsley. Serves 8.

FRESH CORN SALAD

6 ears corn, husked
2 large tomatoes, chopped
1 small green pepper, cut into strips
1/2 cup green onions, minced
3/4 cup HERB DRESSING p. 170

Steam the corn until tender; set aside to cool. Cut the kernels off the cobs with a sharp knife and combine with the remaining ingredients; toss and adjust the seasoning. Chill well before serving on a bed of lettuce. Garnish with fresh parsley, tomato wedges or pepper rings. Serves 8.

FRESH FRUIT CUP

2 Tbsp. frozen orange juice concentrate
1 tsp. fresh lemon juice
1 apple, diced
1 orange, peeled and chopped
1 peach, diced
1 banana, sliced
1/2 cup each seedless grapes and blueberries
Any other fruits in season (papaya, mango, grapefruit, etc.), diced or chopped
CURRIED FRUIT DRESSING p. 167, optional
Chopped walnuts and fresh mint

Combine the juices and prepared fruit in a covered bowl; mix well and chill until ready to serve. Top with the dressing, if desired, and garnish with the walnuts and fresh mint. Serves 6-8.

GREEN BEAN ASPIC

1 24-oz. can V-8® or mixed vegetable juice
8 Tbsp. agar-agar flakes
1 tsp. Tabasco® sauce
1/4 cup fresh lemon juice
1 Tbsp. tamari
1/3 cup slivered almonds
1/3 cup chopped celery
1 cup cooked French-style green beans
Sea salt and pepper to taste
Romaine lettuce leaves
TOFU MAYONNAISE p. 147

In a medium saucepan, bring the V-8® juice and agar-agar to a boil. Lower the heat and simmer for about 5 minutes, stirring continuously; set aside to cool. Add the Tabasco® sauce, lemon juice and tamari; chill until the mixture has thickened slightly. Meanwhile, toast the almonds in a toaster oven or in a heavy skillet over medium heat, stirring continuously. Remove the slightly thickened aspic from the refrigerator; stir in the celery, green beans and toasted almonds. Season to taste and pour into a 4-cup gelatin mold; refrigerate for several hours until firm. When ready to serve, invert the mold onto a bed of lettuce leaves and serve with TOFU MAYONNAISE. Serves 4.

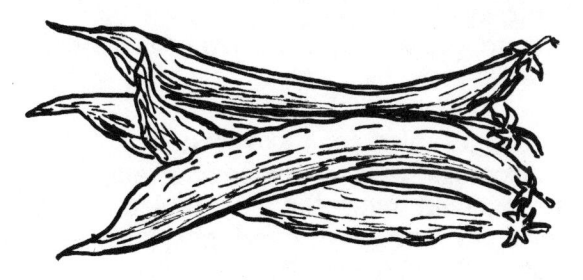

JERUSALEM ARTICHOKE SALAD

6 Jerusalem artichokes, grated
2 carrots, grated
3 stalks celery, finely chopped
1/4 cup chopped fresh parsley
1/2 cup TOFU MAYONNAISE p. 147 (more to taste)
Sweetener to taste
Lettuce leaves
1/4 cup sliced black olives and a sprig of parsley

Prepare the vegetables and set aside. Combine the parsley, TOFU MAYONNAISE and sweetener; toss with the vegetables. Serve on a bed of lettuce leaves and garnish with black olives and parsley. Serves 6.

MIDDLE EASTERN SLAW

1 1/2 cups shredded cabbage
3/4 cup each sliced carrots and celery
10 whole black olives
1/4 cup chopped fresh parsley
1/4 cup each cider or rice vinegar, lemon juice and
    vegetable stock
1 clove garlic, crushed
A pinch of tarragon, optional
1/8 tsp. cayenne pepper and 1/2 tsp. sea salt

Place all the vegetables in a covered bowl. Mix the herbs and seasonings with the vinegar, lemon juice and vegetable stock; pour over the vegetables and toss. Cover and marinate at least overnight, basting occasionally. Makes 3 1/2 cups.

POTATO-PECAN SALAD

5 cups diced cooked potatoes
1 cup TOASTED BUTTER PECANS p. 11
1/2 cup chopped celery
1/4 cup chopped sweet red peppers
1/4 cup chopped fresh parsley
EASY SESAME p. 168 or MISO DRESSING I p. 171

Combine all the ingredients in a large mixing bowl and toss gently until well coated with the dressing of choice. Serve on a bed of lettuce leaves. Serves 8.

POTATO-VEGETABLE SALAD

5 cups cubed potatoes
1 medium carrot, diced
1 cup fresh or frozen green peas
6 stalks celery, sliced
3 green onions, including tops, sliced
1 Tbsp. powdered vegetable broth
1 cup MUSTARD DRESSING p. 172
Sea salt and pepper to taste

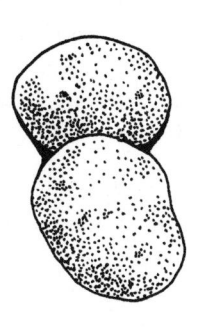

Place the potatoes and carrots in a large pot and steam until almost tender; add the peas and finish steaming. Cool and drain; save the water to use later as vegetable stock. In a large mixing bowl, combine the cooled vegetables with the celery and green onions. Add the MUSTARD DRESSING and toss gently until well coated; sprinkle with paprika and garnish with a sprig of fresh parsley. Serves 6-8.

STUFFED BEETS

8 fresh medium-sized beets
2 Tbsp. oil
2 Tbsp. lemon juice or wine vinegar
1 tsp. Dijon-style mustard
Sea salt and pepper to taste
1/2 cup sour cream or LOW-FAT "SOUR CREAM" p. 145
1 1/2 Tbsp. prepared horseradish, drained
1/2 tsp. Dijon-style mustard

Wash the beets well and cook, unpeeled, in salted, boiling water for 30 minutes. Cool, peel and level off the bottom of the beets so that they will stand up straight. Scoop out the center of each beet, leaving a shell about 1/4-inch thick. Save the beet centers and chop finely to use in the stuffing. Mix the oil, lemon, 1 tsp. mustard, salt and pepper together and marinate the beets in this dressing for about 1 hour, turning frequently. Meanwhile, combine the sour cream, horseradish, 1/2 tsp. mustard and chopped beet centers; season to taste and mix well. Just before serving, drain the beets; fill the centers with the sour cream mixture. Serve 2 stuffed beets on a bed of lettuce for each person. Serves 4.

SUMMER GARDEN SALAD

1 cup sliced celery
1 cup cubed cucumber
1/2 cup green pepper rings, cut in half
1/2 cup diced sweet red pepper
8 Chinese pea pods, cut in 1-inch lengths
1/4 cup sliced radishes
1/4 cup sliced red onions, cut in half
ITALIAN DRESSING p. 170

Combine all the ingredients and toss; chill and serve on a bed of lettuce leaves. Serves 8.

TANGY APPLE MOLD

1/2 cup agar-agar flakes
2 cups HOMEMADE APPLESAUCE p. 184
1 cup carbonated water
1 tsp. grated orange peel
1/4 cup orange juice concentrate
1 cup chopped apple and 1/4 cup chopped walnuts
2 Tbsp. fresh lemon juice
TOFU MAYONNAISE p. 147
Lettuce and fresh watercress

In a saucepan, heat the applesauce and agar-agar; simmer for 5 minutes. Remove from the heat and cool. Stir in the carbonated water, orange juice and peel; chill until partially set. Toss the chopped apple and walnuts in the lemon juice; add to the applesauce mixture and turn into a 4- or 5-cup ring mold. Chill until firmly set; unmold on lettuce leaves. Top with TOFU MAYONNAISE and garnish with watercress. Serves 6-8.

TOMATOES WITH BASIL

3-4 tomatoes, cut into wedges
1/2 tsp. dried or 1 tsp. chopped fresh basil
1/2 cup ITALIAN DRESSING p. 170

Combine the basil and ITALIAN DRESSING; mix well. Pour over the tomato wedges, toss and chill. Marinate for several hours, tossing frequently. When ready to serve, spoon onto a bed of lettuce. Serves 6-8.

TROPICAL WALDORF SALAD

SALAD:
4 apples, cored and diced
1 cup crushed pineapple
1/2 cup chopped walnuts
1 cup chopped celery
1/2 cup raisins
1/2 cup diced mango or papaya

SAUCE:
1 cup TOFU MAYONNAISE p. 147
2 Tbsp. black cherry or apricot concentrate
2 Tbsp. frozen, unsweetened apple juice concentrate
1/4 tsp. sea salt

Combine all the salad ingredients and toss. Add the sauce; toss again and chill for at least 1 hour before serving. Serves 6-8.

VEGETABLE ASPIC

2 Tbsp. oil
1/2 cup chopped onion
1 28-oz. can peeled, crushed tomatoes
1 bay leaf
1 clove of garlic, minced or 1/8 tsp. garlic powder
1/4 tsp. paprika
1/2 cup agar-agar flakes
2 Tbsp. tamari
1 Tbsp. cider or rice vinegar
Juice and grated peel from 1/2 lemon
1/2 cup diced green pepper
1/2 cup grated carrot
1/2 cup chopped celery
1/2 cup chopped cucumber, radishes, olives or any other vegetables
Sea salt and pepper to taste
Small bunch of watercress

In a large skillet, heat the oil and sauté the onions until transparent. Add the tomatoes, bay leaf, garlic and paprika; cook gently for 10 minutes. Add the agar-agar to the tomato mix, and continue to cook for about 5 more minutes, stirring continuously. Add the tamari, vinegar, lemon peel and juice and chopped vegetables; season to taste. Pour into a large oiled ring mold and cool; chill in the refrigerator for several hours. When ready to serve, turn the aspic out of the mold onto a bed of lettuce, and fill the center with fresh watercress. Serve with TOFU MAYONNAISE p. 147 or MISO DRESSING II p. 171. Serves 6-8.

WATERCRESS AND GREEN BEAN SALAD

1 medium potato, cooked and diced
1 lb. fresh string beans, cooked and cut in 1-inch pieces
1 large bunch watercress, trimmed and chopped
1/2 medium red onion, thinly sliced
1 medium cucumber, thinly sliced
1 cup sliced mushrooms
1 cup "SOUR CREAM" DRESSING p. 172
Sea salt and pepper to taste

Combine all the vegetables in a large bowl. Add the "SOUR CREAM" DRESSING; toss and season to taste. Serve on a bed of romaine lettuce. Serves 6-8.

WATERCRESS-SPROUT SALAD

1 cup watercress
4 romaine lettuce leaves
1 cup alfalfa sprouts
1/4 cup GOMASIO p. 144 (toasted ground sesame seeds)
1/4 cup grated carrots
MISO or CREAMY GARLIC DRESSING p. 166

Remove the thick stems from the watercress. Tear or cut the lettuce into bite-sized pieces. Combine all the ingredients and toss gently until well coated with the dressing of choice. Serves 4.

SALAD DRESSINGS

AVOCADO DRESSING

1 cup TOFU MAYONNAISE p. 147
1 small avocado
1 tsp. chopped onion or 1/4 tsp. onion powder
1 clove garlic, minced or 1/4 tsp. garlic powder
1/8 tsp. cayenne pepper, optional
1 Tbsp. fresh lemon juice, optional
1/4-1/2 cup vegetable stock
Sea salt and pepper to taste

Combine all the ingredients in a blender or food processor and process until smooth. Serve over a vegetable salad. (To use as a dip, omit the vegetable stock and serve with a FRESH VEGETABLE PLATTER p. 6.) Makes about 2 cups.

COLESLAW DRESSING

1/2 cup plain yogurt
1/4 cup TOFU MAYONNAISE p. 147
1/4 cup unsweetened pineapple juice
2 Tbsp. apple juice concentrate
2 Tbsp. lemon juice
1/4 tsp. celery seed
1/4 tsp. sea salt
Freshly ground pepper to taste

Combine all the ingredients in a screw-top jar and shake; chill for several hours and shake again before serving over COLESLAW p. 153. Makes 1 cup.

CREAMY CURRY DRESSING

2 tsp. curry powder
1/2 cup oil
1/2 cup fresh lemon juice
1/3 cup TOFU MAYONNAISE p. 147
1 clove garlic, minced or 1/4 tsp. garlic powder
1 tsp. chopped onion
1/8 tsp. cayenne pepper, optional
1 tsp. apple juice concentrate
Sea salt and pepper to taste

Whisk all the ingredients together until smooth and toss with the RICE-WALNUT SALAD p. 140 or salad greens. Makes about 1 cup.

CREAMY GARLIC DRESSING

1 cup TOFU MAYONNAISE p. 147
1 clove garlic, minced or 1/4 tsp. garlic powder
1 tsp. Italian herbs
1 Tbsp. chopped fresh parsley
1/2 tsp. herb seasoning salt or 1/4 tsp. sea salt
Freshly ground pepper to taste
Vegetable stock to thin

Combine all the ingredients in a blender or food processor and blend until smooth; add the vegetable stock as needed, to thin. Chill for several hours and serve over salad greens. Makes 1 1/2 cups.

CUCUMBER DRESSING

1 1/2 cups chopped cucumber
3/4 cup TOFU MAYONNAISE p. 147
2 Tbsp. chopped green onions
1 Tbsp. fresh lemon juice
1/2 tsp. dill weed
1/2 tsp. herb seasoning salt or 1/4 tsp. sea salt
Vegetable stock to thin

Combine all the ingredients in a blender or food processor and blend until smooth; add the vegetable stock as needed, to thin. Chill for several hours and serve over salad greens. Makes 2 cups.

CURRIED FRUIT DRESSING

1 cup TOFU MAYONNAISE p. 147
1/3 cup apple juice concentrate
1/3 cup mashed peaches, nectarines or plums
1/2 tsp. curry powder
1/2 tsp. grated lemon peel
1/8 tsp. sea salt
1/8 tsp. cayenne pepper

Combine all the ingredients in a blender or food processor and blend well. Chill for several hours before serving to blend the flavors. Serve over APPLE-TANGERINE SALAD p. 150, FRESH FRUIT CUP p. 156 or other fruit salads. Makes 1 3/4 cups.

CURRIED TOMATO DRESSING

3/4 cup tomato juice
1/4 cup oil
3 Tbsp. fresh lime or lemon juice
1/2 tsp. grated fresh ginger
1/2 tsp. curry powder
1/4 tsp. cayenne pepper
1 Tbsp. chopped fresh parsley
1/4 cup chopped green onions
1 tsp. PEANUT BUTTER p. 10
1/8 tsp. ground cumin
1/8 tsp. sea salt

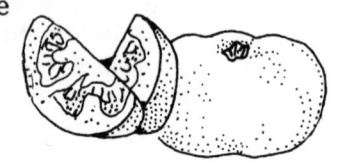

Combine all the ingredients in a screw-top jar and shake; chill for several hours and shake again before serving over salad greens. Makes 1 cup.

EASY SESAME DRESSING

1/2 cup oil
1/3 cup fresh lemon juice (more to taste)
2 tsp. chopped fresh parsley
1 tsp. mixed Italian herbs
1 Tbsp. GOMASIO p. 144
Herb seasoning salt or sea salt to taste

Combine all the ingredients in a screw-top jar with an ice cube; shake well. Remove the ice cube and serve. Makes about 3/4 cup.

FRENCH LEMON DRESSING

1/2 cup oil
1/4 cup fresh lemon juice
1 tsp. grated lemon peel
1 Tbsp. cider or rice vinegar
1 tsp. dry mustard
1 tsp. apple juice concentrate
1/8 tsp. sea salt
1/8 tsp. ground white pepper

Combine all the ingredients in a screw-top jar; shake well and chill. Shake again before serving over salad greens. Makes 1 cup.

GREEN GODDESS DRESSING

1 cup chopped fresh parsley
2 green onions with tops, chopped
1/2 cup plain yogurt
1 cup TOFU MAYONNAISE p. 147
2 Tbsp. lemon juice
1/2 tsp tarragon
1/2 tsp. dill
Sea salt to taste (or garlic salt)
Vegetable stock to thin

Combine all the ingredients in a blender or food processor and blend until smooth; add the vegetable stock as needed, to thin. Chill and serve over salad greens. Makes 2 cups.

HERB DRESSING

1/3 cup lemon juice
1/3 cup oil
1/2 tsp. dry mustard
1/8 tsp. cayenne pepper
1 Tbsp. minced chives or green onions
1 Tbsp. minced fresh parsley
1 small clove garlic, minced
1/2 tsp. basil
1/4 tsp. tarragon
1/2 tsp. sea salt
Freshly ground black pepper to taste

Combine all the ingredients in a screw-top jar; shake well and chill before serving. Makes 3/4 cup.

ITALIAN DRESSING

1/3 cup fresh lemon juice
1/2 cup oil
2 Tbsp. water
1/2 tsp. mixed Italian herbs
1/8 tsp. granulated kelp
1/2 tsp. powdered vegetable broth
1/8 tsp. onion powder
1/8 tsp. garlic powder
Sea salt or herb seasoning salt and pepper to taste

Combine all the ingredients in a screw-top jar; shake well and chill before serving. Use as a salad dressing or marinade for cooked or raw vegetables. Makes about 3/4 cup.

MISO DRESSING I

1/2 cup oil
1/2 tsp. sesame oil (toasted, if available)
1/3 cup lemon juice or cider or rice vinegar
1/3 cup white miso or 1/4 cup red, barley or hatcho miso
1 clove garlic, minced
1/4 tsp. dried or 1/2 tsp. grated fresh ginger
1/4 tsp. dry mustard
1/4 cup vegetable stock

Combine all the ingredients in a screw-top jar and shake; chill well and shake again before serving. Makes 1 cup.

MISO DRESSING II

1/3 cup miso
1/3 cup tahini
1/4 cup lemon juice
1/4 cup vegetable stock
1 clove garlic, minced or
    1/4 tsp. garlic powder

Whisk all the ingredients together until smooth and chill well before serving. Makes 1 1/4 cups.

MUSTARD DRESSING

1 cup TOFU MAYONNAISE p. 147 or plain yogurt
1 1/2 Tbsp. Dijon-style mustard
1 tsp. prepared horseradish
1/4 cup vegetable stock to thin
1/4 tsp. herb seasoning salt or 1/8 tsp. sea salt
1/8 tsp. ground white pepper

Whisk all the ingredients together until smooth and chill well before serving. Makes 1 1/4 cups.

"SOUR CREAM" DRESSING

1 cup TOFU MAYONNAISE p. 147
1/4 cup fresh lemon juice
2 tsp. cider or rice vinegar
1/2-1 tsp. sea salt
1 tsp. dried or 2-3 tsp. fresh dill weed
Freshly ground pepper to taste
3 Tbsp. sweetener (rice syrup or apple juice
    concentrate), optional

Whisk all ingredients together until completely blended. Serve on WATERCRESS AND GREEN BEAN SALAD p. 164 or other vegetable salads. Makes about 1 1/2 cups.

Sandwich Combinations

SANDWICH COMBINATIONS

1. ALMOND BUTTER p. 2 and apple slices.

2. ANDREA'S VEGETARIAN CHILI p. 91, olive slices, topped with Cheddar cheese and toasted.

3. BANANA-DATE NUT BUTTER p. 2.

4. BEAN BURRITO p. 92 and HOT TACO SAUCE p. 189, topped with cheese and heated.

5. CASHEW BUTTER p. 2, mixed with raisins, topped with banana slices.

6. CURRIED CASHEW SPREAD p. 5, sliced tomato and onion, topped with alfalfa sprouts.

7. FALAFEL p. 96, MIDDLE EASTERN SLAW p. 158, chopped tomatoes and TAHINI SAUCE p. 195.

8. GREAT NORTHERN BEAN SPREAD p. 7, sliced tomato and alfalfa sprouts.

9. HOMMUS p. 9, mixed with chopped fresh spinach, topped with sliced cucumber and red onion.

10. HOMMUS p. 9, sliced avocados and olives, and fresh spinach leaves.

11. HOMMUS p. 9, sliced tomato and cucumber, topped with alfalfa sprouts.

12. LENTIL-VEGIE LOAF p. 101, lettuce, sliced tomato and onion, and NUTTY CHEESE SAUCE p. 192.

13. LENTIL-VEGIE LOAF p. 101, lettuce, sliced
    tomato, and TAHINI SAUCE p. 195.

14. MOCK or LOW-FAT "CREAM CHEESE" p. 145-6,
    apple slices and chopped watercress.

15. MOCK or LOW-FAT "CREAM CHEESE" p. 145-6,
    mixed with chopped nuts and dried apricots.

16. MOCK or LOW-FAT "CREAM CHEESE" p. 145-6,
    mixed with chopped green onions, topped with thinly sliced radishes.

17. MOCK or LOW-FAT "CREAM CHEESE" p. 145-5,
    mixed with chopped olives and walnuts.

18. MOCK or LOW-FAT "CREAM CHEESE" p. 145-6,
    mixed with chopped pimentos, topped with sliced onion.

19. MOCK or LOW-FAT "CREAM CHEESE" p. 145-6,
    watercress and sliced tomato.

20. MOCK or LOW-FAT "SOUR CREAM" p. 145-6,
    mixed with chopped peaches, apples and walnuts.

21. MOCK or LOW-FAT "SOUR CREAM" p. 145-6,
    mixed with chopped watercress, topped with tomato and cucumber slices.

22. MOCK or LOW-FAT "SOUR CREAM" p. 145-6,
    mixed with grated, cooked beets and topped with sliced onion and sprouts.

23. MOCK or LOW-FAT "SOUR CREAM" p. 145-6,
    mixed with sautéed mushrooms, topped with alfalfa sprouts.

24. MOCK or LOW-FAT "SOUR CREAM" p. 145-6, sliced avocado, tomato and onion.

25. PEANUT BUTTER p. 10, mixed with chopped olives and celery, topped with grated carrots and sliced onion.

26. PEANUT BUTTER p. 10, mixed with grated carrots and seedless raisins.

27. PEANUT BUTTER p. 10, topped with grated carrots and sliced bananas.

28. PEANUT BUTTER p. 10, topped with thinly sliced cucumber and tomato.

29. Puréed pinto beans, mixed with HOT TACO SAUCE p. 189, layered with sliced tomato and onion, topped with shredded cheese and toasted.

30. SOY "SAUSAGE" p. 112 patties, lettuce, sliced tomato, and HUNGARIAN SAUCE p. 190.

31. TAHINI SAUCE p. 195, sliced tomato and onion, topped with Cheddar cheese and toasted.

32. Tahini (sesame butter) and DRIED FRUIT JAM p. 183.

33. TOFU CROQUETTES p. 117, lettuce, sliced tomato, sprouts and SPICY PEANUT SAUCE p. 193.

34. TOFU MAYONNAISE p. 147 and BAKED BEANS p. 216, topped with sliced onion.

35. TOFU MAYONNAISE p. 147, mashed avocado, a squeeze of lemon and sliced onion.

36. TOFU MAYONNAISE p. 147, asparagus, sliced tomato and alfalfa sprouts.

37. TOFU MAYONNAISE p. 147, mixed with finely chopped onions and celery, topped with alfalfa sprouts.

38. TOFU MAYONNAISE p. 147, mixed with grated carrots, chopped celery and sliced olives.

39. TOFU MAYONNAISE p. 147, mixed with horseradish and mustard, layered with lettuce and slices of onion, cooked beets, cucumber, tomato and green pepper.

40. TOFU MAYONNAISE p. 147, mixed with horseradish, layered with sliced avocado and tomatoes, topped with alfalfa sprouts.

41. TOFU MAYONNAISE p. 147, mixed with shredded cabbage and grated carrot, layed with onion and green pepper rings, topped with sliced cheese.

42. TOFU MAYONNAISE p. 147, SCRAMBLED TOFU I or II, p. 52, topped with sliced tomato and onion.

43. TOFU MAYONNAISE p. 147, sliced LENTIL-VEGIE LOAF p. 101, lettuce, sliced tomato and cucumber.

44. TOFU MAYONNAISE p. 147 and thin apple slices, topped with sliced Cheddar cheese and toasted.

45. TOFU MAYONNAISE p. 147, TOFU BURGER p. 115, HOT TACO SAUCE p. 189, lettuce and sliced tomato, topped with sprouts.

46. TOFU MAYONNAISE p. 147, TOFU FRITTERS p. 119, lettuce, sliced tomato and HOT TACO SAUCE p. 189.

47. TOFU MAYONNAISE p. 147, TOFU TURKEY p. 125 and CRANBERRY RELISH p. 183.

48. TOFU MAYONNAISE p. 147, 3-4 slices of MARINATED TOFU p. 102, layered with shredded zucchini, onion rings, sliced tomato and mushrooms, topped with cheese and heated.

49. TOFU "RICOTTA CHEESE" p. 148, mixed with grated radish, topped with sliced green pepper rings.

50. TOFU ROAST p. 122, sliced onion and MUSHROOM GRAVY p. 191.

51. TOFU EGG(LESS) SALAD I p. 118, sliced tomato and lettuce.

52. TOFU EGG(LESS) SALAD II p. 118, sliced tomato and lettuce.

53. TOFU EGG(LESS) SALAD III p. 119, alfalfa sprouts and lettuce.

54. TOFU SLOPPY JOES p. 123, sliced olives and onion, and lettuce.

55. TOFU STEAK p. 123, sliced tomato, and sprouts.

Sauces

SWEET SAUCES

Almond Cream, 180
Apple Sauce, 180
Banana Sauce, 181
Blueberry Sauce, 181
Cashew Cream, 182
Cherry Sauce, 182
Cranberry Relish, 183
Dried Fruit Jam, 183
Ginger Yogurt, 184
Homemade Apple-
  sauce, 184
Raisin Sauce, 184
Sesame-Coconut
  Cream, 185
Strawberry Sauce, 186

SAVORY SAUCES

Cashew "Hollandaise"
  Sauce, 187
Catsup, 187
Gravy I, 188
Gravy II, 188
Hot Taco Sauce, 189
Hungarian Sauce, 190
Italian Tomato Sauce, 190
Mexican Tomato Sauce, 191
Mushroom Gravy, 191
Mushroom-Soy Pasta
  Sauce, 192
Nutty Cheese Sauce, 192
Spicy Peanut Sauce, 193
Sweet and Spicy Miso
  Gravy, 194
Tahini Sauce, 195
Watercress Sauce, 195
White Sauce, 196

SWEET SAUCES

ALMOND CREAM

1/2 cup blanched almonds
1/2 cup water
2 pitted dates or dried figs
1/4 tsp. orange juice concentrate
Pinch of sea salt

In a food processor or blender, chop the almonds to a fine powder; add the remaining ingredients and process until smooth. Serve in place of dairy cream, over fruit, pies or grains. Makes 1 cup.

APPLE SAUCE

2 cups apple juice
2 Tbsp. cornstarch, potato starch or arrowroot
2 Tbsp. butter or soy margarine
1/2 tsp. vanilla extract
Pinch of cinnamon, optional

In a small saucepan, bring 1 3/4 cups of the apple juice to a boil. Dissolve the potato starch or arrowroot in the remaining 1/4 cup of apple juice and add to the boiling juice, stirring continuously until thickened. Remove from the heat, and stir in the butter and vanilla extract. Serve warm, over APPLE UPSIDE-DOWN CAKE p. 73, FRUIT AND NUT TURNOVERS p. 33 or any breakfast pancake, waffle, muffin or biscuit. Makes about 2 cups.

BANANA SAUCE

2 cups NUT MILK p. 23 or coconut milk
2 very ripe bananas
1/2 tsp. vanilla extract
1/8 tsp. sea salt
1-2 Tbsp. frozen orange juice concentrate
3 Tbsp. agar-agar flakes

Blend the "milk," bananas, vanilla, salt and orange juice concentrate in a blender or food processor until smooth. Pour into a saucepan; add the agar-agar and bring to a boil, stirring continuously. Chill well and serve on pancakes or waffles. Makes about 2 1/2 cups.

BLUEBERRY SAUCE

2 cups fresh or frozen unsweetened blueberries
1/2 cup water or apple-blueberry juice
2 Tbsp. sweetener (maple syrup, fruit juice
    concentrate, rice syrup, etc.)
1 tsp. fresh lemon juice, optional
2 Tbsp. cornstarch or potato starch or arrowroot

Bring the blueberries, water and sweetener to a boil; reduce the heat and simmer until the berries pop open. Remove from the heat; cool and blend in a food processor or blender until smooth. Return to the saucepan; heat again. Dissolve the starch or arrowroot in a little cold water and add to the sauce, stirring continuously until thickened. Stir in the lemon juice and serve on muffins, pancakes, waffles or FRUIT AND NUT TURNOVERS p. 33. Makes about 2 cups.

CASHEW CREAM

1/2 cup cashews
1/2 cup water
1 Tbsp. sweetener (maple syrup, apple juice concentrate, rice syrup, or 2 pieces of dried fruit)
1/4 tsp. vanilla extract
Pinch of sea salt

In a food processor or blender, chop the cashews to a fine powder; add the remaining ingredients and process until smooth. Serve as you would dairy cream, over fruit, pies or grains. Makes 1 cup.

CHERRY SAUCE

1 16-oz. can unsweetened sour cherries
1/2 cup frozen apple juice concentrate
2 Tbsp. black cherry concentrate
2 Tbsp. cornstarch, potato starch or arrowroot
1/4 cup apple juice

Rinse and drain the cherries; purée in a food processor with the apple and black cherry concentrates. Transfer the purée to a saucepan and bring to a boil; reduce the heat. Dissolve the potato starch or arrowroot in the apple juice and add it to the purée, stirring continuously until the mixture thickens. Serve hot or cold on pancakes and waffles, as a spread for muffins or biscuits and on FRUIT AND NUT TURNOVERS p. 33.
Makes about 2 cups.

CRANBERRY RELISH

1 cup cranberries, stemmed and finely chopped
1 apple, cored and finely chopped
1/4 cup water
1/4 cup frozen orange juice concentrate
1/4 cup frozen apple juice concentrate
1 Tbsp. agar-agar flakes

Combine all the ingredients in a small saucepan and simmer for about 5 minutes. Set aside to cool. Refrigerate overnight to blend the flavors and serve cold with CRANBERRY-NUT BREAD p. 32 or TOFU TURKEY p. 125. Makes 2 cups.

DRIED FRUIT JAM

2 cups mixed dried fruit
1 cup hot water
2 Tbsp. orange juice concentrate
1 tsp. grated lemon rind

In a saucepan, bring the fruit and water to a boil; cover and set aside to soak until soft, about 30 minutes. Place all the ingredients in a blender or food processor and blend until smooth. Serve on toast, muffins, or sandwiches. Makes about 3 cups.

GINGER YOGURT

2 cups plain yogurt
1 heaping Tbsp. grated fresh ginger
2 Tbsp. maple syrup
1/2 tsp. lemon juice, optional

Combine all the ingredients; mix well, and chill. Serve as a topping for pancakes, waffles, or fresh fruit. Makes about 2 cups.

HOMEMADE APPLESAUCE

6 baking apples
1/2 cup raisins
1/2 cup apple juice
1 tsp. cinnamon
A squeeze of fresh lemon juice

Core and chop the apples; place in large saucepan with the remaining ingredients. Bring to a boil and simmer until well done. Serve with toast, pancakes or waffles or as a main meal side dish. Makes about 3 cups.

RAISIN SAUCE

2 cups raisins
1 cup boiling water (or more to cover)
Ground pecans or walnuts and/or coconut

Place the raisins in a screw-top jar; cover with the boiling water and allow to stand overnight. Or boil the raisins in the water for a few minutes until plump. Place the plump raisins, and just enough water to process, in blender or food processor; blend until smooth and add the nuts and/or coconut to thicken. Serve for breakfast over cereal, brown rice, waffles, or pancakes; or for dessert over fruit crepes, fruit-nut breads or FRUIT AND NUT TURNOVERS p. 33. Makes about 3 cups.

SESAME-COCONUT CREAM

1/2 cup sesame seeds
1/2 cup grated fresh coconut (or dried, unsweetened coconut)
1 tsp. sweetener (maple or rice syrup, apple juice concentrate, etc.)
1/8 tsp. sea salt
1 cup boiling water

Grind or finely chop the sesame seeds in a food processor. Add the remaining ingredients and blend well. The cream may be strained or diluted with more water, if desired, and served over breakfast cereal or in recipes calling for sweet cream. Makes about 3 cups.

STRAWBERRY SAUCE

1/2 cup strawberry concentrate
2 Tbsp. maple syrup
2 cups sliced strawberries
2 Tbsp. potato starch, cornstarch or arrowroot
1/4 cup apple juice

Place the strawberry concentrate, maple syrup and strawberries in a small saucepan; bring to a boil. Dissolve the starch or arrowroot in the apple juice and add to the strawberries. Reduce the heat and stir continuously until the sauce has thickened. Serve over pancakes, waffles, biscuits or FRUIT AND NUT TURNOVERS p. 33. Makes about 2 cups.

SAVORY SAUCES

CASHEW "HOLLANDAISE" SAUCE

3 Tbsp. butter or soy margarine
3 Tbsp. rice flour
1 1/2 cups CASHEW MILK p. 17
1/3 cup lemon juice
1/8 tsp. cayenne pepper (more to taste)
Sea salt to taste

Melt the butter in a medium-sized saucepan on low heat. Add the flour and mix well. Slowly add the cashew milk, stirring until the mixture is quite thick and creamy. Remove from the heat. Add the lemon juice, cayenne pepper and salt; mix well. Serve over steamed vegetables or crepes. Makes about 1 3/4 cups.

CATSUP

1 6-oz. can tomato paste
1 Tbsp. rice or cider vinegar
2 Tbsp. apple juice concentrate
1/2 tsp. herb seasoning salt or to taste
1 Tbsp. liquid soy protein
Paprika and/or cinnamon to taste, optional

Combine all the ingredients and mix well. Serve in place of the grocery store variety which contains sugar and preservatives. Makes 1 cup.

GRAVY I

3 cups vegetable stock
3 Tbsp. tamari or liquid soy protein
3 Tbsp. butter or soy margarine
1/4 tsp. basil
1/8 tsp. marjoram
3 Tbsp. potato starch or cornstarch
Sea salt and pepper to taste
Squeeze of lemon juice

In a small saucepan, combine the vegetable stock, tamari, butter and herbs, and simmer gently for about 5 minutes. Dissolve the starch in a little cold water and add to the gravy, stirring continuously, until thickened. Add the lemon juice, and season to taste. Serve with TOFU TURKEY p. 125, TOFU ROAST p. 122, or any loaf or burger recipes. Makes 3 cups.

GRAVY II

1/4 cup finely chopped onion
2 Tbsp. oil
2 peeled tomatoes, coarsely chopped
2 cups vegetable stock
1/4 cup tamari
Pinch of dried thyme
1 bay leaf
1/4 cup red wine
1 tsp. powdered vegetable broth
Freshly ground pepper to taste
1 Tbsp. arrowroot or potato starch

Continued next page...

Sauté the onion in the oil until golden brown; add the tomatoes and cook, stirring continuously until the liquid has evaporated. Add 1 1/2 cups of the vegetable stock and the herbs and seasonings; simmer for about 20 minutes, stirring occasionally. Remove the bay leaf and purée the gravy in a food processor or blender; reheat. Dissolve the arrowroot or potato starch into the remaining vegetable stock and add to the tomatoes, stirring continuously until thickened. Serve with TOFU TURKEY p. 125, TOFU ROAST p. 122, or any loaf or burger recipes. Makes about 2 cups.

HOT TACO SAUCE

1/2-1 Jalapeño pepper (more to taste), minced
2 small mild chilies, chopped
1 small onion, chopped
6 medium tomatoes, peeled and chopped
5 cilantro (fresh coriander leaves), minced
1/4 cup chopped parsley
Sea salt to taste

UNCOOKED (to serve as a dip):
Combine all the ingredients and mix together well. Season to taste; chill and serve with chips. Makes about 2 cups.

COOKED (to use a sauce):
Sauté the chopped Jalapeño pepper, chilies and onions until tender; add the tomatoes, cilantro, parsley and simmer about 15-20 minutes. Season to taste and use as a sauce over BEAN BURRITOS p. 92 or in other recipes. Makes about 2 cups.

HUNGARIAN SAUCE

1 cup MOCK or LOW-FAT "SOUR CREAM" p. 145-6
1 Tbsp. paprika
1 Tbsp. chili sauce

Combine all the ingredients and mix well. Serve over burgers, loaves, or sandwiches. Makes 1 cup.

ITALIAN TOMATO SAUCE

1 medium onion, chopped
2 Tbsp. oil
1 6-oz. can tomato paste
2 28-oz. cans tomatoes or 4 lb. fresh tomatoes
1/8 tsp. garlic powder or
    1 clove fresh garlic, minced
1 1/2 tsp. mixed Italian herbs (or 1/2 tsp. each basil, thyme, and oregano)
1/4 cup butter or soy margarine
Sea salt and pepper to taste

Sauté the onion in the oil until tender; add the herbs. Purée the tomato paste and tomatoes in a blender or food processor. In a large saucepan, combine the onion mix and puréed tomatoes; bring to a boil. Add the butter, salt and pepper; reduce the heat and simmer for at least 1 hour. (Cook half of a fresh carrot in the sauce to remove any bitterness.) Serve on PIZZA SUPREME p. 107 or pasta. Makes 1 1/2-2 quarts.

MEXICAN TOMATO SAUCE

1 28-oz. can tomato purée
1/2 cup sautéed onion and green peppers
1/2 cup HOT TACO SAUCE p. 189
1/4 cup butter or soy margarine
1/2 tsp. chili powder
1/2 tsp. ground cumin
Sea salt and pepper to taste

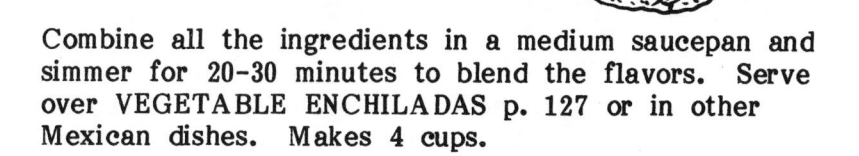

Combine all the ingredients in a medium saucepan and simmer for 20-30 minutes to blend the flavors. Serve over VEGETABLE ENCHILADAS p. 127 or in other Mexican dishes. Makes 4 cups.

MUSHROOM GRAVY

1 lb. mushrooms
2 Tbsp. butter or soy margarine
2 Tbsp. tamari
2 Tbsp. lemon juice
2 Tbsp. potato starch or arrowroot
1/2 cup cold vegetable stock or water

Soak the mushrooms in water for a few minutes (to absorb as much water as possible); then slice. Melt the butter in a saucepan, and sauté the mushrooms until tender. Add the tamari and lemon juice and stir. Dissolve the starch or arrowroot in the vegetable stock and add to the mushrooms, stirring continuously until thickened. Serve as a gravy for burgers, loaves or sandwiches. Makes about 3 cups.

MUSHROOM-SOY PASTA SAUCE

1 large onion, chopped
2 garlic cloves, minced
1/2 lb. mushrooms, sliced
1/4 cup butter or soy margarine
2 28-oz. cans tomato purée
1/2 tsp. basil
1/4 tsp. each oregano, thyme, and marjoram
1 cup textured vegetable protein
Tamari or sea salt and pepper to taste

In a large pot, sauté the onions, garlic and mushrooms in the butter. Add the tomato purée and herbs; mix well. Stir in the soy granules, tamari or salt and pepper; simmer for 30 minutes. Serve over spaghetti, LASAGNA p. 98 or steamed vegetables. (Double the recipe and freeze half for a quick meal later.) Makes 2 quarts.

NUTTY CHEESE SAUCE

1 Tbsp. butter or soy margarine
1 Tbsp. brown rice flour
1 cup CASHEW MILK p. 17
1 cup grated Cheddar cheese
1 Tbsp. tamari
1 tsp. bottled hot sauce or 1/8 tsp. cayenne pepper
1/4 tsp. horseradish
1 tsp. Dijon-style mustard
1 cup finely ground toasted almonds
1 Tbsp. apple juice concentrate

Continued next page...

In a small saucepan, melt the butter and stir in rice flour to form a paste; add the cashew milk, stirring continuously until thickened. Add the Cheddar cheese and continue to heat until the cheese is melted. Stir in the remaining ingredients, until all the flavors are blended. A little extra cashew milk or water may be added to thin the sauce. Serve over steamed cauliflower or broccoli. Makes about 3 cups.

SPICY PEANUT SAUCE

2 Tbsp. potato starch or arrowroot
1/4 cup lemon juice
1/2 cup roasted peanuts
2 cups water or vegetable stock
1 Tbsp. rice or cider vinegar
1 Tbsp. grated ginger root
1/2 Tbsp. cayenne pepper
1/2 Tbsp. ground cumin
1/8 tsp. caraway seeds
1/8 tsp. ground cardamom
1/8 tsp. ground coriander
1/8 tsp. garlic powder
1/2 cup tamari
1/4 cup sesame oil

Dissolve the potato starch in the lemon juice and set aside. Finely grind the peanuts in a food processor and combine with the remaining ingredients in a large saucepan. Simmer for about 10 minutes to blend the flavors; add the lemon juice mixture, stirring continuously until thickened. Serve over TOFU CROQUETTES p. 117, burgers or loaves. Makes about 3 1/2 cups.

SWEET AND SPICY MISO GRAVY

2 green onions, chopped
1 Tbsp. butter or soy margarine
2 Tbsp. raisins
3 cups vegetable stock
3-4 Tbsp. potato starch or arrowroot
3 Tbsp. miso
2 Tbsp. tamari or 3 Tbsp. liquid soy protein
1/2 tsp. powdered vegetable broth
Pinch of garlic powder
1 Tbsp. bottled hot sauce or 1/8 tsp. cayenne pepper
2 Tbsp. apple juice concentrate, optional

In a large saucepan, sauté the green onions in the butter until tender. Add the raisins and 2 1/2 cups of the vegetable stock; simmer for 10 minutes. Dissolve the potato starch or arrowroot and the miso in 1/2 cup of the vegetable stock; add with the remaining ingredients to the stock mixture, stirring continuously until thickened. This unusual gravy goes well with brown rice (even for breakfast) and makes a good marinade for tofu. Makes about 3 cups.

TAHINI SAUCE

1 cup tahini (sesame butter)
1/2 cup lemon juice
1 clove garlic, minced or 1/4 tsp. garlic powder
1/2-1 tsp. sea salt
1/2 cup cold water

In a small bowl, combine the tahini, lemon juice, garlic and salt; slowly beat in the water until the mixture is a thick sauce. Adjust the seasoning and serve with FALAFEL p. 96 in a pita sandwich, or over steamed vegetables and rice. Makes about 2 cups.

WATERCRESS SAUCE

1 cup chopped watercress
4 Tbsp. oil
2 tsp. Dijon-style mustard
2 Tbsp. lemon juice, cider or rice vinegar
1 cup LOW-FAT "SOUR CREAM" p. 145
Sea salt and pepper to taste

Blend all the ingredients in a food processor or blender until smooth. Serve over grains, salads or with ASPARAGUS CREPES p. 92. Makes 1 1/2 cups.

WHITE SAUCE

2 Tbsp. butter or margarine
2 Tbsp. flour (unbleached, whole wheat, rice, etc.)
1 cup milk or NUT MILK p. 23
Sea salt and freshly ground pepper to taste

Melt the butter in a small saucepan over low heat; stir in the flour until well blended. Add the milk, stirring continuously, until thick and smooth. Season to taste; add a variation if desired and blend until smooth. Serve immediately. Makes about 1 cup.

VARIATIONS:
1. 1/2 cup grated cheese of choice for "au gratin" dishes.
2. 1/4 tsp. nutmeg, cayenne, paprika or curry powder.
3. 1 cup sautéed sliced mushrooms.
4. 1/4 cup toasted slivered almonds.
5. 1/4 tsp. dry mustard, 1/2 tsp. grated onion and 1/2 tsp. Worcestershire (without anchovies) sauce.
6. 1 Tbsp. mixed dried parsley, chives, fennel, basil, chervil or tarragon.

Soups

SOUPS

Cabbage-Apple Soup, 198
Cold Cucumber-Yogurt
  Soup, 198
Corn Chowder, 199
Cream of Asparagus
  Soup, 200
Cream of Broccoli
  Soup, 201
Gail's Gumbo, 202
Gazpacho, 203
Green Miso Soup, 204
Hot and Sour Soup, 204
Lentil Soup, 205
Mixed Bean Soup, 206
Mushroom-Barley Soup, 207
Mushroom-Potato Soup, 208
Peanut Butter Soup, 208
Russian Borscht, 209
Spicy Vegetable Soup, 210
Split Pea Soup, 211
Summer Beet Soup, 212
V-8® Vegie Soup, 212
White Gazpacho Soup, 213
Zucchini Soup, 214

CABBAGE-APPLE SOUP

1 small onion, chopped
1 clove garlic, minced or 1/4 tsp. garlic powder
3 cups shredded cabbage
2 Tbsp. butter or soy margarine
5 cups vegetable stock or water
1 potato, diced
2 apples, cored and chopped
1 1/2 cups chopped tomatoes
1 tsp. herb seasoning salt or 1/2 tsp. sea salt
Freshly ground pepper to taste
Prepared mustard, optional

In a large soup pot, sauté the onions, garlic and cabbage in the butter until tender. Add the remaining ingredients and simmer (do not boil) for 30 minutes. Serves 6-8.

COLD CUCUMBER-YOGURT SOUP

4 cucumbers, grated
6 cups plain yogurt
1 cup vegetable stock or water
3 cloves garlic, crushed
4 Tbsp. oil
2 Tbsp. cider or rice vinegar
1 Tbsp. dried or 2 Tbsp. fresh dill, minced
1 tsp. sea salt

Combine all the ingredients; mix and chill well before serving. Garnish with a cucumber slice or fresh parsley sprig in each bowl. Serves 6.

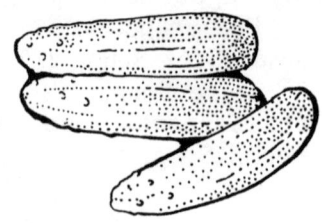

CORN CHOWDER

2 Tbsp. butter or soy margarine
1 small onion, chopped
1/2 cup chopped celery
1/2 cup chopped sweet red pepper or pimentoes
2 Tbsp. flour
3 cups vegetable stock
2 cups corn kernels
2 cups cubed potatoes
2 cups NUT MILK p. 23
1/8 tsp. ground nutmeg
2 tsp. herb seasoning salt or 1 tsp. sea salt
Freshly ground pepper to taste

In a large saucepan, sauté the onions, celery and red peppers in the butter until tender; add the flour to form a paste and brown lightly. Stir in the stock, corn, and potatoes and simmer until the potatoes are tender, about 20 minutes. Stir in the NUT MILK and seasoning; simmer (do not boil) for 10 more minutes, stirring frequently. Adjust the seasoning and garnish with chopped red pepper or pimentoes. Serves 4.

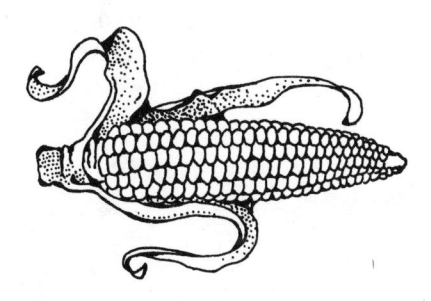

CREAM OF ASPARAGUS SOUP

1 1/2 lb. fresh asparagus
2 cups reserved water from the steamed asparagus
1/4 cup butter or soy margarine
1/3 cup flour
1 cup milk or NUT MILK p. 23
1/4 tsp. lemon balm or summer savory
1 tsp. herb seasoning salt or 1/2 tsp. sea salt
Freshly ground pepper to taste

To prepare the asparagus for cooking: Hold the tip end in one hand and the stem end in the other; bend each asparagus spear until it breaks. Use only the tip ends and discard the tough stems; steam until tender and reserve the liquid. Cut off the extreme tips of the steamed asparagus and set aside to use later. Blend the remaining stems until smooth in a food processor or blender (use a little reserved stock as necessary).

Meanwhile, make a white sauce by melting the butter in the bottom of a saucepan; stir in the flour to form a paste and add the NUT MILK, stirring continuously until the sauce thickens. Add the blended asparagus stems, the remainder of the reserved stock, the asparagus tips and the lemon balm or savory; heat slowly, stirring continuously (do not boil). Season to taste and serve with a garnish of fresh lemon balm or parsley. Serves 4.

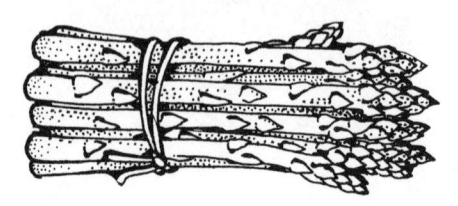

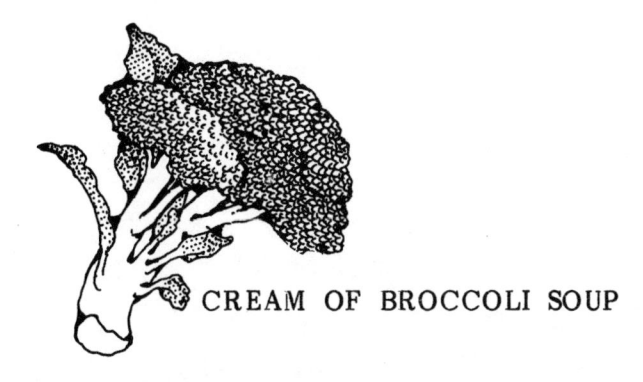

CREAM OF BROCCOLI SOUP

1 head fresh broccoli
1 fresh fennel root, optional
1 cup reserved water from the steamed broccoli
1/4 cup butter or soy margarine
1/3 cup flour
2 cups milk or NUT MILK p. 23
Pinch of sage
Sea salt and cayenne pepper to taste

Remove the broccoli flowerettes from the stems and set aside. Peel the tough, thick stems and cut into 1-inch pieces. If fresh fennel root is available, discard the green part and cut the root into small pieces. Steam the broccoli stems and fennel until almost tender; add the broccoli flowerettes and steam a few more minutes. Remove the flowerettes and set aside; reserve the liquid and combine with the stems and root in a blender or food processor; purée until smooth.

Meanwhile, make a white sauce by melting the butter in the bottom of the saucepan and stirring in the flour to form a paste. Add the NUT MILK, stirring continuously over low heat until the sauce thickens. Add the puréed stems and root, the remainder of the reserved stock, the broccoli flowerettes and the sage; heat slowly, stirring continuously (do not boil). Season to taste and serve with HERB CROUTONS p. 144.
Serves 4.

GAIL'S GUMBO

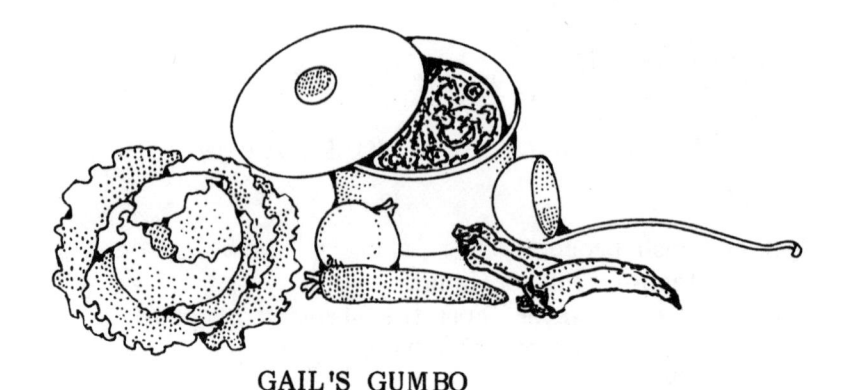

1 1/2 cups okra (fresh or frozen)
4 cups tomato juice
2 cups water
1 cup Chinese peapods (fresh or frozen)
2 cups shredded cabbage
1 cup chopped carrots
1/2 cup chopped onion
1/2 cup chopped celery
1 tsp. dried or 2 tsp. chopped fresh basil
1 bay leaf
1/2 tsp. ground white pepper
1/2 tsp. ground cumin
2 Tbsp. tamari
Sea salt and freshly ground pepper to taste

Slice the okra into 1-inch pieces and set aside. In a large saucepan, bring the tomato juice and water to a boil. Add the remaining ingredients; reduce the heat and simmer for about 1 hour. Add the okra and continue to simmer for 15 more minutes; adjust the seasoning and serve. Serves 6-8.

GAZPACHO

SOUP:
2 cloves garlic, crushed
6 very ripe medium tomatoes, peeled and chopped
1 medium cucumber, peeled and chopped
1 large green pepper, chopped
1/4 cup lemon juice or cider or rice vinegar
2 cups tomato juice
1/4 cup oil
1/2 tsp. sea salt
Freshly ground black pepper and cayenne pepper to taste

CONDIMENTS:
1 cucumber, sliced
1/2 cup chopped green onions
1/2 cup chopped green pepper
1/4 cup chopped radish
1/4 cup chopped celery
1 cup HERB CROUTONS p. 144

Combine the garlic, tomatoes, cucumber, green pepper and lemon juice or vinegar in a food processor or blender and process until smooth. Add the tomato juice, oil, and seasonings; mix well. Chill well before serving in individual bowls; garnish with the condiments. Serves 6.

GREEN MISO SOUP

1 Tbsp. sesame oil (toasted, if available)
4 green onions, sliced
1/4 lb. tofu, cut in 1/2-inch cubes
5 cups water
1 cup chopped spinach, (fresh or frozen)
1 carrot, sliced
1/4 cup miso

In a soup pot, sauté the green onions and tofu cubes in the sesame oil. Add the water, spinach and carrots; bring to a boil. Reduce the heat and cover. Simmer until the vegetables are just tender, 20-30 minutes. Remove from the heat. Dissolve the miso in about 1/4 cup of the soup broth and stir into the soup; cover and set aside for about 5 minutes before serving. Serves 4.

HOT AND SOUR SOUP

2 quarts water
1 lb. fresh spinach, washed and chopped
1/2 small cabbage, shredded
2 stalks celery, sliced diagonally
1 carrot, thinly sliced
6 green onions, sliced
1 hot pepper, minced
Sea salt or tamari to taste
Freshly ground black pepper to taste
Cayenne pepper to taste
1/4 cup lemon juice

Continued next page...

Place all the ingredients except the lemon juice in a large pot; bring to a boil, reduce the heat and simmer, covered, for about 30 minutes (until the carrots are tender). Stir in the lemon juice and set aside for about 5 minutes. Garnish with chopped parsley, sliced green onions or crisp noodles. Serves 8.

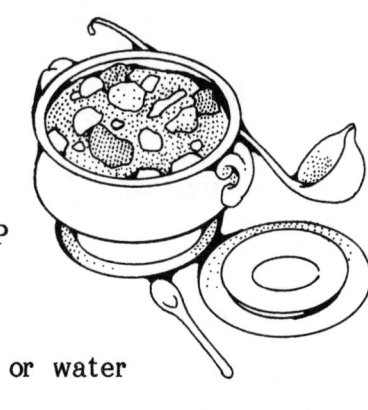

LENTIL SOUP

2 cups lentils
2 quarts hot vegetable stock or water
2 medium potatoes, cubed
2 carrots, cubed
1/2 lb. fresh or frozen spinach, chopped
1 Tbsp. chopped, fresh parsley
1 clove garlic, minced
1/2 tsp. dried or 1 tsp. chopped fresh basil
1/2 cup chopped onion
1/4 cup chopped green onions
1 bay leaf
1 6-oz. can tomato paste, optional
Sea salt and freshly ground pepper to taste
1/4 cup butter or soy margarine or to taste

Wash the lentils well (be sure to remove any stones); set the butter aside. Combine the lentils and stock with the remaining ingredients; simmer for at least 1 hour until the vegetables are tender and the flavors are blended. Add the butter; mix well. Serves 8-10.

MIXED BEAN SOUP

1/2 cup each of six different dried beans (pinto, kidney, navy, lima, garbanzo, Great Northern, adzuki, or black beans)
1 1/2 quarts water for soaking
5 cups vegetable stock or water for cooking
1 cup chopped onion
1/2 cup chopped green peppers
1/2 cup sliced celery
1/2 cup sliced carrots
1 clove garlic, minced
1 bay leaf
1/2 tsp. marjoram
1 tsp. basil
1/2 tsp. summer savory
1/8 tsp. thyme
1/4 cup tamari
1 Tbsp. powdered vegetable broth
1 cup chopped tomatoes
1/2 tsp. sea salt
2-3 Tbsp. butter or soy margarine

Rinse the beans well and soak overnight in the 1 1/2 quarts of water. When ready to cook, rinse again and drain; cook until tender (see DRIED BEANS p. 94). Add the remaining ingredients and pressure-cook or simmer until the vegetables are tender. Remove 2 cups of the beans and vegetables and purée in a blender or food processor. Return the purée to the soup and add the butter; mix well and simmer about 10 more minutes. Serves 8-10.

MUSHROOM-BARLEY SOUP

1 medium onion, chopped
2-3 stalks celery, cut into 1-inch pieces
3 carrots, cut into 1-inch pieces
1 lb. mushrooms, sliced
1 cup barley
2 1/2 quarts vegetable stock or water
Sea salt or tamari and freshly ground pepper to taste
Fresh parsley, chopped

In a covered pot, steam the celery, carrots and 1/3 of the mushrooms until tender; then purée in a food processor, adding vegetable stock as needed. Sauté the onion and the rest of the mushrooms until tender. Place the vegetable purée, sautéed mixture and the rest of the stock in a large pot; add the barley and season to taste. Cook on low heat about 1 1/2 hours (the longer it cooks, the better it tastes and the thicker it gets). Garnish with chopped parsley and serve. (Use leftovers as gravy for TOFU STEAK p. 123.) Serves 8.

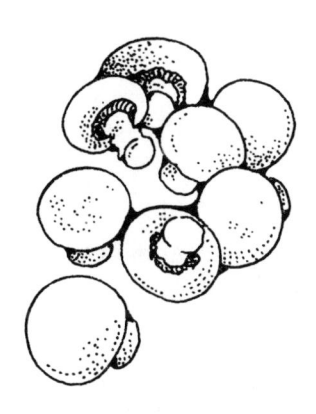

MUSHROOM-POTATO SOUP

1/2 lb. mushrooms, sliced
1/2 cup each sliced onion and celery
2 Tbsp. butter or soy margarine
1 lb. potatoes, thinly sliced
1 bay leaf and 1 tsp. dried parsley
1 large carrot, sliced
1 tsp. powdered vegetable broth
3 cups vegetable stock
Sea salt and freshly ground pepper to taste
LOW-FAT "SOUR CREAM" p. 145, optional

Set the sour cream aside. In a large pot, sauté the mushrooms, onion and celery in the butter until tender. Add the remaining ingredients; simmer for 20 minutes. Season to taste; serve with a spoonful of sour cream in each bowl. Serves 4.

PEANUT BUTTER SOUP

1 medium onion, chopped
1 cup chopped celery
2 Tbsp. oil
1/4 cup PEANUT BUTTER p. 10
1 1/2 cups vegetable stock
2 cups tomato juice
1/2 tsp. ground coriander
1/8 tsp. ground white pepper and sea salt to taste
1 tsp. powdered vegetable broth
Plain yogurt, optional

Continued next page...

In a large saucepan, sauté the onion and celery in the oil until tender. Stir the peanut butter into the sautéed mixture; add the vegetable stock, tomato juice and seasonings. Bring to boil and simmer for 10 minutes. Serve in individual bowls, topped with a spoonful of yogurt. Serves 4.

RUSSIAN BORSCHT

1 lb. fresh beet roots
4 cups vegetable stock
4 medium potatoes, sliced
1 medium onion, sliced
2 small carrots, sliced
2 stalks celery, sliced
1 bay leaf
1 large ripe tomato, peeled and wedged
Sea salt and freshly ground pepper to taste
LOW FAT "SOUR CREAM" p. 145, optional

Peel and thinly sice the beets; place with the vegetable stock in a large soup pot. Bring to a boil; reduce the heat and simmer for 15 minutes. Add the potatoes, onions, celery and carrots (add more vegetable stock, if necessary). Cook for 15 more minutes; add the bay leaf, tomatoes and seasonings. Cook until all the vegetables are tender. Serve hot with a spoonful of sour cream in each bowl. Serves 4-6.

SPICY VEGETABLE SOUP

5 medium potatoes, diced
2 carrots, diced
1 lb. fresh green beans, cut into 1/2-inch pieces
1 cup fresh or frozen peas
1 small onion, chopped
1/2 small head cabbage, shredded
1 16-oz. can whole tomatoes
1/2 cup HOT TACO SAUCE p. 189 or 2 small hot
  peppers, finely chopped
Water to cover the vegetables
Sea salt or herb seasoning salt and pepper to taste
3 Tbsp. butter or soy margarine, optional

Place all the ingredients except the butter in a pressure cooker and cook for 10 minutes; or a soup pot and simmer for 45 minutes. Stir in the butter, adjust the seasoning and serve. Serves 6-8.

SPLIT PEA SOUP

2 pkg. dried split peas
3 quarts vegetable stock or water
3 carrots, cut into 1-inch pieces
3-4 medium potatoes, cut into quarters
1 medium onion, optional
1/4 cup butter or soy margarine
1/8 tsp. dried basil (or dill or oregano, if preferred)
Sea salt and freshly ground pepper to taste
HERB CROUTONS p. 144

IN CROCK POT: Wash the peas well, carefully removing any stones, and place in a crock pot. Add the vegetable stock, potatoes, carrots, onion and basil. Cook on low heat overnight or all day. About 15 minutes before serving, remove the vegetables and blend them in a food processor until smooth. Return the purée to the soup and add the butter, salt and pepper; thin with more vegetable stock, if necessary. Simmer another 15 minutes and serve with HERB CROUTONS.

IN LARGE SOUP POT: Wash the peas, carefully removing any stones, and place in the pot. Add the vegetable stock and bring to a rolling boil; cut off heat and let soak for at least 1 hour. Add the potatoes, carrots, onions and seasonings; simmer until the peas are thick and "mushy." About 15 minutes before serving, remove the vegetables; purée them in a food processor or blender, then return to the soup pot. Add the butter, salt and pepper and thin with more vegetable stock, if necessary. Simmer for 15 more minutes and serve with HERB CROUTONS. Serves 8-10.

SUMMER BEET SOUP

2 green onions and tops, sliced
1 cup vegetable stock
2 1/2 cups chopped cooked beets
1 1/2 cups buttermilk
2 Tbsp. lemon juice
1 Tbsp. dried or 2 Tbsp. snipped fresh chives
1/4 tsp. dried or 1/2 tsp. snipped fresh dill weed
1/2 tsp. ground white pepper

In a small saucepan, simmer the onions in the stock until tender; place in a food processor with the remaining ingredients and blend until smooth. Chill for 2 hours and garnish with fresh dill. Serves 4.

V-8® VEGIE SOUP

48-oz. can V-8® Juice or a mixed vegetable juice
1 small onion, chopped
2 carrots, sliced
2 stalks celery, sliced
6 new potatoes, diced
Handful of cauliflowerettes, green beans, shredded cabbage and/or any other raw or leftover vegetables
1/8 tsp. basil
1/4 tsp. parsley
1/8 tsp. garlic powder or 1 crushed garlic clove
Water to cover vegetables

Place all ingredients in a large pot and simmer until the vegetables are tender, about 30 minutes. Serve with a garnish of chopped, fresh parsley. Serves 6-8.

WHITE GAZPACHO SOUP

SOUP:
1 cup thinly sliced green onions and tops
2 cloves garlic, minced
3 Tbsp. butter or soy margarine
3 cups milk or NUT MILK p. 23
2 tsp. powdered vegetable broth
1 large potato, cooked and cubed
1 Tbsp. lime juice
1/2 tsp. bottled hot pepper sauce (more to taste)
1/4 tsp. ground cumin
1 tsp. sea salt
1/2-1 tsp. ground white pepper

CONDIMENTS:
Chopped green pepper
Sliced green onion
Chopped tomato
Sliced mushrooms
Chopped cucumber
Chopped watercress

Sauté the green onions and garlic in the butter until tender. Dissolve the powdered vegetable broth in the milk and stir it into the onions; simmer until the flavors are blended. Stir in the remaining soup ingredients. Transfer the mixture to a blender or food processor and blend until smooth; refrigerate overnight or until thoroughly chilled, at least 2 hours. Serve the soup in individual bowls and the condiments on a platter for everyone to help themselves. Serves 4.

ZUCCHINI SOUP

6 small zucchini, cut into chunks
1 large onion, thinly sliced
1 tsp. curry powder
1/2 tsp. ground ginger
1/2 tsp. dry mustard
1 tsp. powdered vegetable broth
3 cups vegetable stock
3 Tbsp. uncooked brown rice
1 1/2 cups milk or NUT MILK p. 23
Sea salt and freshly ground pepper to taste
Minced chives for garnish

Combine the zucchini, onion, curry powder, ginger, mustard and powdered vegetable broth in a saucepan; add the vegetable stock and rice and bring to a boil. Cover and simmer for 45 minutes. Transfer the mixture to a blender or food processor and purée; add the milk and season to taste. Reheat (do not boil); serve hot or cold. Garnish with minced chives. Serves 6.

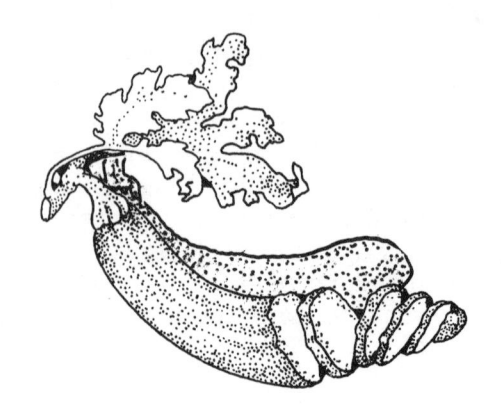

Vegetables

Baked Beans, 216
Baked Celery, 216
Braised Endive, 217
Broccoli Hollandaise, 217
Broccoli San
  Vincente, 218
B R's Endive
  Potatoes, 218
Brussels Sprouts
  Creole, 219
Cabbage-Walnut
  Sauté, 219
Carrot Bake, 220
Carrot-Stuffed Butternut
  Squash, 220
Cream Corn with
  Chives, 221
French Green Beans with
  Almonds, 221
Fresh Kale (Turnip or
  Collard Greens), 222
Fried Okra, 222
Gingered Jerusalem
  Artichokes, 223
Green Beans and Red
  Peppers, 223
Green Beans Oregano, 224
Green Beans with Water
  Chestnuts, 224
Sautéed Bean
  Sprouts, 225

Sautéed Parsnips and
  Carrots, 225
Spaghetti Squash, 226
Steamed Artichokes, 226
Stewed Okra, 227
Stuffed Mushrooms, 227
Summer Squash
  Casserole, 228
Vegetable Stew, 229
Wax Beans Almondine, 229
Yellow Squash with
  Onions, 230
Zucchini Bake, 230

BAKED BEANS

3 cups cooked Great Northern beans
2 Tbsp. molasses
2 Tbsp. apple juice concentrate
1/2 cup tomato paste
1/4 cup lemon juice
2 Tbsp. rice or cider vinegar
1 Tbsp. chili powder
1/8 tsp. garlic powder
1/2 tsp. tamari
1/4 tsp. onion powder
1 cup vegetable stock

Combine all the ingredients in a baking dish and mix well; bake at 350°F. for about 1 hour. Serves 6.

BAKED CELERY

1 whole head celery, washed
1 Tbsp. oil
1 tsp. sesame oil
1 Tbsp. lemon juice
1 Tbsp. tamari
6 green onions, chopped

Place the oils and the whole celery head in the bottom of a covered baking dish. Sprinkle the lemon juice and tamari over the celery; cover and bake at 350°F. for 30 minutes. Add the green onions to the celery and bake for another 15 minutes. Serves 4.

BRAISED ENDIVE

4 Tbsp. butter or soy margarine
10 small heads fresh Belgian endive (about 3 lb.)
1/2 tsp. powdered vegetable broth
Sea salt and freshly ground pepper to taste
2 Tbsp. lemon juice

Wash the endive, separate the leaves and cut into 1-inch pieces. Melt the butter in a skillet and add the endive, powdered vegetable broth, salt and pepper. Mix well and simmer for 20 minutes, covered. Uncover and sprinkle with the lemon juice; toss and serve. Serves 6.

BROCCOLI HOLLANDAISE

1 large head broccoli
CASHEW "HOLLANDAISE" SAUCE p. 187

Break or cut the broccoli into bite-sized pieces and place in steamer basket in a large pot; add water to cover bottom of pot (about 1-inch high or more, if you want to save the stock for later). Bring to a boil, cover, reduce the heat and simmer until the broccoli is tender-crisp. Meanwhile, prepare the "HOLLANDAISE" sauce. Place the steamed broccoli in a heated serving dish, cover with the sauce, and serve. Serves 6-8.

BROCCOLI SAN VINCENTE

1 large head broccoli, cut into bite-sized pieces
1 pint sour cream, or LOW-FAT "SOUR CREAM" p. 145
1 cup rennetless Cheddar cheese, finely shredded
1 tsp. grated lemon rind
2 Tbsp. lemon juice
1/4 tsp. sea salt
Freshly ground pepper to taste
1/2 cup slivered almonds, toasted

Steam the broccoli until just tender and place in a shallow baking dish. Combine the remaining ingredients and spoon over the broccoli. Place under the broiler about 5 inches from the heat and broil about 3 minutes, until the cheese begins to melt. Remove from the broiler and serve immediately. Serves 4-6.

B R's ENDIVE POTATOES

8 cups chopped new potatoes (unpeeled)
1 cup chopped onion
6 Tbsp. butter or soy margarine
4 cups chopped fresh Belgian endive
1/4 cup tamari

Boil the potatoes for mashing. Sauté the onions and endive in the butter until tender and add with the tamari to the potatoes (still hot). Mash everything together and serve as a side dish or use as a stuffing for TOFU ROAST p. 122. Serves 6.

BRUSSELS SPROUTS CREOLE

4 cups Brussels sprouts
1/4 cup chopped onion
1/4 cup chopped green pepper
1/4 cup chopped sweet red pepper
1/4 cup chopped celery
2 Tbsp. oil
1 clove garlic, minced or 1/4 tsp. garlic powder
2 cups diced fresh tomatoes
Herb seasoning salt or sea salt and freshly ground
    pepper to taste
1/4 tsp. poultry seasoning
Cayenne pepper or hot sauce to taste

Clean the Brussels sprouts and soak for 20 minutes in cold salted water; drain and set aside. In a large skillet, sauté the onion, green and red peppers and celery in the oil. Add the remaining ingredients; cover and simmer for 20 minutes. Serves 6.

CABBAGE-WALNUT SAUTE

1 cup walnut pieces
3 Tbsp. butter or soy margarine
1/2-1 head cabbage, shredded
1/4 tsp. caraway seeds
Sea salt and freshly ground pepper to taste

Skillet-toast the walnuts in the butter until golden. Remove from the pan; then add the cabbage and caraway seeds and sauté until tender. Season with salt and pepper; add the walnuts, toss and serve. Serves 6.

CARROT BAKE

3 cups grated carrots
3 Tbsp. butter or soy margarine
Sea salt and freshly ground pepper to taste
Sprinkle of cinnamon, optional

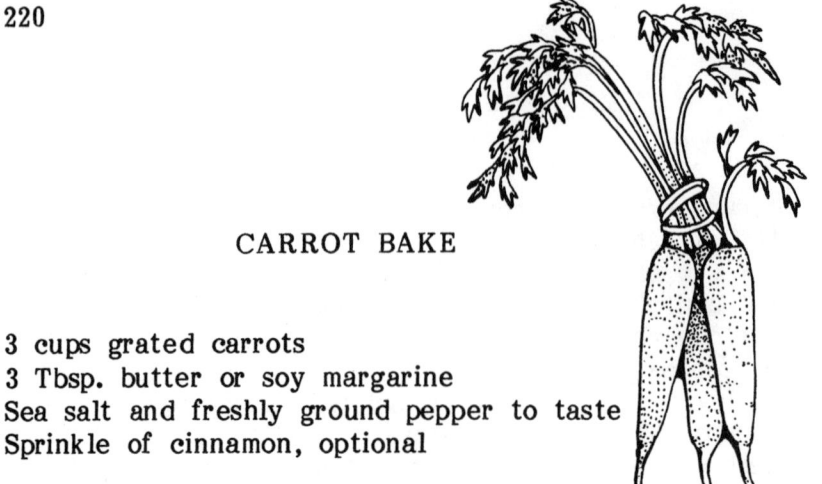

Bake the shredded carrots in a tightly covered 1-quart casserole dish at 325°F. for 30 minutes. (Do not add water.) Remove from the oven, add the butter and seasonings and serve immediately. Serves 6.

CARROT-STUFFED BUTTERNUT SQUASH

2 small butternut squash
1 cup grated carrots
1/4 cup raisins
1/4 cup orange juice
Pinch of cinnamon, optional
4 tsp. butter or soy margarine

Cut the butternut squash into halves, remove the seeds and set aside. Combine the grated carrots, raisins, orange juice and cinnamon and stuff into the squash cavities. Place the squash halves in a baking pan and dot with butter. Bake uncovered at 350°F. for 40 minutes, or until tender. Serves 4.

CREAMED CORN WITH CHIVES

1/2 cup MOCK or LOW-FAT "CREAM CHEESE" p. 145
1/4 cup vegetable stock
2 tsp. chopped chives
2 cups cooked corn kernels
Sea salt and freshly ground pepper to taste
Paprika

Heat the "cream cheese" and the vegetable stock over low heat, stirring constantly. Add the chives and corn; heat thoroughly, stirring occasionally. Season to taste; serve in a heated dish and sprinkle with paprika. Serves 4.

FRENCH GREEN BEANS WITH ALMONDS

2 lb. green beans
1 cup blanched, slivered almonds
1 tsp. thyme
1/2 tsp. sweet marjoram
3 Tbsp. butter or soy margarine

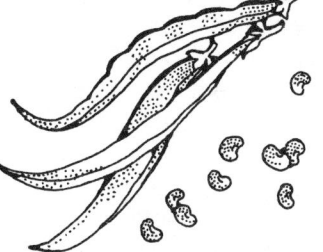

Wash and slice the string beans diagonally. Steam the beans until just tender. Toast the almonds until golden brown. Place the beans in a covered casserole dish, dot with butter and sprinkle with the herbs and almonds. Serve immediately. Serves 6-8.

FRESH KALE (TURNIP OR COLLARD GREENS)

4 lb. fresh kale or other greens, washed and chopped
1/4 cup butter or soy margarine
3 Tbsp. powdered vegetable broth
1 tsp. herb seasoning salt or 1/2 tsp. sea salt
1-2 Tbsp. lemon juice

Steam the kale until tender, about 15 minutes. Add the remaining ingredients, mix well and place in a heated serving bowl. (If fresh greens are not available, frozen kale may be substituted.) Serves 6.

FRIED OKRA

1 lb. fresh okra, sliced in 1/2-inch pieces
1 egg or equivalent egg replacer
Rice flour, seasoned with sea salt and freshly ground pepper to taste
Oil for deep-fryer

Coat the okra slices with the egg or egg replacer; then roll in the flour and seasoning mix. Deep-fry a few at a time until golden brown. Drain on paper towels and place in the oven to keep warm until all are fried. Serves 4.

GINGERED JERUSALEM ARTICHOKES

1 lb. fresh Jerusalem artichokes, cut bite-sized
2 Tbsp. grated fresh ginger
3 Tbsp. butter or soy margarine
1 tsp. powdered vegetable broth

Steam the artichokes until just tender. Melt the butter in a small saucepan and sauté the ginger; stir in the powdered vegetable broth (dilute with vegetable stock if needed). Add the steamed artichokes and toss gently; serve immediately. Serves 4-6.

GREEN BEANS AND RED PEPPERS

1 1/2 lb. green beans
1/2 cup chopped onion
1 sweet red pepper, diced
1 Tbsp. chopped parsley
3 Tbsp. butter or soy margarine
1 tsp. powdered vegetable broth
Sea salt and freshly ground pepper to taste

Preheat the oven to 375°F. Wash and snap the beans into 1-inch pieces; place half of the beans in a buttered baking dish with a tight-fitting cover. Layer with half of the onion, red pepper, parsley, powdered vegetable broth, salt, and pepper; dot with butter. Make a second layer of the beans, vegetables and seasonings; cover and bake for 40 minutes. Serves 6-8.

GREEN BEANS OREGANO

2 lb. fresh green beans, cut into
    1-inch lengths
3 tomatoes, cut into small wedges
1 small onion, sliced
1/4 cup chopped celery
1/4 cup chopped green pepper
1/8 tsp. ground white pepper
1/4 tsp. oregano

Place all the ingredients in a large non-stick skillet. Add 1/4 cup of water, cover and simmer, stirring occasionally, until the beans are tender, about 15 minutes. Serves 6-8.

GREEN BEANS WITH WATER CHESTNUTS

2 lb. fresh green beans, cut in 1-inch pieces
1 8-oz. can water chestnuts, sliced
3 Tbsp. butter or soy margarine
1/4 cup tamari
1/4 cup lemon juice

Steam the beans until tender-crisp. Meanwhile, melt the butter and sauté the water chestnuts for a few minutes. Add the tamari and lemon juice and mix well. Add the cooked beans, toss and serve. Serves 6-8.

SAUTEED BEAN SPROUTS

1/4 cup oil
6 green onions, sliced
1 clove garlic, minced
2 lb. mung bean sprouts, washed
1/4 cup tamari or 1/3 cup liquid soy protein
1 Tbsp. sherry, optional
1 Tbsp. sesame oil (toasted, if available)
Sea salt or herb seasoning salt to taste

Heat the oil in a wok or large skillet; stir-fry the green onions and garlic for about 1 minute over high heat. Add the bean sprouts, tamari and sherry; stir-fry for 5 minutes. Add the sesame oil; season and toss again. Serve in a heated serving dish. Serves 6-8.

SAUTEED PARSNIPS AND CARROTS

1/2 lb. carrots, cut into julienne strips
1/2 lb. parsnips, cut into julienne strips
1/4 cup plain yogurt
1 Tbsp. fresh parsley, minced
2 tsp. minced fresh dill or 1 tsp. dried dill
2 Tbsp. butter or soy margarine (skip this step if
    serving cold as a salad)
Sea salt and freshly ground pepper to taste

Steam the carrots for about 5 minutes; add the parsnips and steam until tender. Combine the remaining ingredients and set aside. When the vegetables are cooked, drain and stir in the yogurt mixture. Serve hot or cold. Serves 4.

SPAGHETTI SQUASH

Place 1 large spaghetti squash on an oiled baking dish; bake at 350°F. for 1 hour or until tender. Cut the squash in half lengthwise and scoop out the seeds. Then empty the shells with a fork, gently pulling out the spaghetti-like squash threads. If the threads do not come out easily, turn each half over in a baking dish with a little water and bake 15-20 minutes longer. Use in SPAGHETTI SQUASH CASSEROLE p. 113 or serve with tomato sauce, or a sauce of melted butter and summer savory. Serves 8.

STEAMED ARTICHOKES

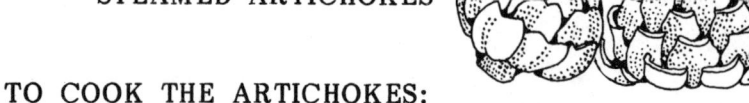

TO COOK THE ARTICHOKES:
Allow one artichoke per person. Wash the artichokes and remove the tough outer leaves. With the scissors, remove the pointy tips of the remaining leaves. Trim off the excess stem, place the artichokes in a steamer basket and steam for about 45 minutes, or until the artichokes are a dull green color and a leaf can be pulled out easily. When cooked, remove the artichokes from the steamer and turn them upside-down to drain. They may be served hot or cold, with a lemon butter sauce or HERB DRESSING p. 170.

TO EAT THE ARTICHOKES:
One leaf at a time is pulled off and dipped into a sauce. The fleshy end at the base of the leaf should be scraped between the front teeth. At the center of the artichoke are some thin prickly leaves and fuzz which should be removed and discarded. The heart at the base of the artichoke is the most delectable part.

STEWED OKRA

1/4 cup oil
3/4 cup chopped onions
1 cup chopped celery
1 cup diced sweet red pepper
2 cups thinly sliced okra
2 cups chopped fresh tomatoes
1 cup vegetable stock or water
Sea salt and cayenne pepper to taste

Sauté the onions, celery and peppers in the oil until tender; add the remaining ingredients. Simmer for 30 minutes; season to taste and serve with rice. Serves 8.

STUFFED MUSHROOMS

3 lb. giant mushrooms
3 stalks celery, chopped
1 small onion, chopped
1 cup pecans (or other nuts), chopped
1 can water chestnuts, chopped
3 1/2 cups breadcrumbs (10 slices whole-grain toast)
1/4 cup. butter or soy margarine
1/8 tsp. basil and/or tarragon
Herb seasoning salt or sea salt and pepper to taste

Clean the mushrooms and chop the stems to use in the stuffing. In a large mixing bowl, combine the chopped stems and the remaining ingredients; mix well. Arrange the mushroom caps in an oiled baking pan. Fill with the stuffing mixture and bake about 15 minutes at 350°F.; then broil for 5 minutes. Makes 2-3 dozen.

SUMMER SQUASH CASSEROLE

2 lb. yellow squash
1/4 cup butter or soy margarine
1/2 tsp. sea salt
1/2 cup TOFU MAYONNAISE p. 147
1/2 cup chopped onion
1/3 cup chopped green pepper
1/4 cup chopped pecans
1/2 cup grated cheese, optional
1/4 cup chopped pimento
3 Tbsp. bread crumbs
Pecan halves for garnish

Steam the squash until tender-crisp and drain. Add the butter and mash. Set the bread crumbs and pecan halves aside. Combine the remaining ingredients and stir into the mashed squash. Pour the mixture into an oiled casserole dish; sprinkle with the bread crumbs and top with the pecan halves. Bake at 350°F. for 35-40 minutes or until browned. Serves 4-6.

VEGETABLE STEW

1/4 cup butter or soy margarine
1/4 head green cabbage, shredded
1/2 onion, chopped
2 small turnips, cubed
2 carrots, sliced
2 medium potatoes, cubed
2 cups vegetable stock
1 Tbsp. ROUX p. 147
1 large tomato, peeled and cut in wedges
2 cloves
1 bay leaf
Sea salt and freshly ground pepper to taste

Melt the butter in a large saucepan. Add the vegetables; mix well and sauté until tender. Add the remaining ingredients, mix well and simmer, covered, for 20 minutes. Serves 6-8.

WAX BEANS ALMONDINE

1 lb. wax beans, cut into 1-inch lengths
3 Tbsp. butter or soy margarine
1/2 tsp. marjoram
1/8 tsp. freshly ground pepper
Herb seasoning salt or sea salt to taste
1/2 cup slivered almonds, toasted

In a large skillet, sauté the beans in the butter until tender-crisp. Stir in the seasonings; add the almonds and serve. Serves 4-6.

YELLOW SQUASH WITH ONIONS

3 Tbsp. butter or soy margarine
2 lb. yellow squash, thinly sliced
1 medium onion, thinly sliced
Herb seasoning salt or sea salt and pepper to taste
Summer savory, optional

Melt the butter in a large skillet and add the remaining ingredients. Cover and sauté until tender-crisp, about 20 minutes, stirring frequently. (Or steam the vegetables.) Season to taste. Serves 6-8.

ZUCCHINI BAKE

4 zucchini squash, sliced
1 medium onion, sliced
1/2 lb. mushrooms
1 sweet red pepper, sliced
2 garlic cloves, minced or 1/2 tsp. garlic powder
1/2 tsp. dried basil or 1 tsp. chopped fresh basil
Olive oil
Tamari or sea salt and freshly ground pepper to taste
Chopped parsley

Place the zucchini in the bottom of an oiled baking dish and arrange the onion, whole mushrooms, red pepper, garlic and basil on top of the zucchini. Sprinkle with a little olive oil, tamari or salt and pepper. Bake at 350°F. for about 20 minutes until the vegetables are tender. Sprinkle with chopped parsley and serve. Serves 6-8.

General Index

Agar-agar flakes (also see Glossary): 77; 82; 83; 85; 146; 155; 157; 161; 163
Almond(s): -apricot cheesecake, 81; butter, 2; butter balls, 59; candy, 59; cookies, 63; cream, 180; milk, 16; nutty cheese sauce, 192; pie crust, 79; wax beans almondine, 229
Almond cream, 180: 71; 72; 76; 77; 88
Almond milk (also see Nut Milk), 16: 51; 81
APPETIZERS, DIPS AND SPREADS: 1-14
Apple(s) (also see Fruit, dried or fresh): baked, 74; cobbler, 82; cabbage-apple soup, 198; cranberry relish, 183; fresh fruit cup, 156; fruit and nut turnovers, 33; homemade applesauce, 184; milk, 16; muffins, 28; spicy fruit pancakes, 53; tangy apple mold, 161; -tangerine salad, 150; upside-down cake, 73
Apricot(s) (also see Fruit, dried or fresh): almond-apricot cheesecake, 81; -corn bread, 28; whole wheat-apricot bread, 38
Arrowroot (see Glossary): used throughout
Artichoke(s): steamed, 226; wild rice-artichoke casserole, 142
Asparagus: cooked vegetable salads, 154; crepes, 92; cream of asparagus soup, 200
Avocado(s): dressing, 165; salad, 150

Banana(s) (also see Fruit, dried or fresh): carob creme pie, 84; cinnamon oatmeal with, 46; -date nut butter, 2; deep-fried, 76; frozen grapes, bananas and strawberries, 70; -nut biscuits, 29; -nut bread, 30; papaya with fruit sherbet, 71; sauce, 181; sherbet, 70; spicy fruit pancakes, 53
Barley (also see Grains; Glossary): -mushroom bake, 132; mushroom-barley soup, 207
Beans (also see Glossary; Dried beans, 94):
General: baked beans, 216; confetti bean salad, 153; mixed bean soup, 206
Black: pie, 93; with soy "sausage," 94
Black-eyed pea(s) or field pea(s): salad, 151; shepherd's pie, 111
Garbanzo: confetti bean salad, 153; cooked vegetable salads, 154; falafel, 96; hommus, 9; Mexican garbanzos, 104
Great Northern: baked beans, 216; spread, 7; shepherd's pie, 111
Green (see Green Beans)
Kidney: Andrea's vegetarian chili, 91; bean burrito, 92; confetti bean salad, 153; vegetable enchiladas, 127
Lima: shepherd's pie, 111
Pinto: bean burrito, 92; vegetable enchiladas, 127
Wax (see Wax beans)

Beets: cooked vegetable salads, 154; horseradish dip, 9; Russian borscht, 209; stuffed, 160; summer beet soup, 212
BEVERAGES: 15-26
Biscuits (see Breads): 27
Black walnuts: 60
Blueberry(ies) (also see Fruit, dried or fresh): -coconut cream pie, 82; fresh fruit cup, 156; fresh fruit pie, 85; fruit and nut turnovers, 33; -mango pudding or pie, 83; -oatmeal waffles, 45; sauce, 181
BREADS: 27-42
BREAKFASTS: 43-56
Broccoli: -cauliflower salad, 152; cream of broccoli soup, 201; hollandaise, 217; Laurie's broccoli-cauliflower casserole, 98; San Vincente, 218
Brown rice (also see Glossary — Grains), 132: about grains, 130; and corn, 133; bulgur-rice, 135; date rice, 47; hardy grain pancakes, 49; homemade cream of rice cereal, 50; kasha-rice cereal, 50; Laurie's broccoli-cauliflower casserole, 98; lentil-stuffed cabbage, 100; lentil-vegie loaf, 101; mushroom-rice ring, 138; Russian cabbage pie, 110; -stuffed cabbage, 108; stuffing, 134; tofu croquettes, 117; tomato rice, 141; -vegetable salad, 139; -walnut salad, 140; wild rice-artichoke casserole, 142
Brussels sprouts: 219

Bulgur (also see Grains; Glossary — Grains): about grains, 130; casserole, 134; nut-fruit tabouli, 138; -rice, 135; tabouli, 140
Buttermilk: biscuits, 30; cornmeal waffles, 47; fig lassi, 18; ginger-nut waffles, 48; low-fat "cream cheese," 145; summer beet soup, 212
Cabbage: -apple soup, 198; coleslaw, 153; Gail's gumbo, 202; hot and sour soup, 204; lentil-stuffed, 100; Middle Eastern slaw, 158; rice-stuffed, 108; Russian cabbage pie, 110; spicy vegetable soup, 210; vegetable stew, 229; -walnut sauté, 219
Calamondin: 74
Candy(ies) (see Desserts): 57
Cantaloupe: 17
Carob (also see Glossary): chip-oatmeal cookies, 64; -coated fresh fruit, 75; creme pie, 84; nutty cookies, 66; -peanut butter fudge, 60
Carrot(s): bake, 220; blended salad, 151; bulgur casserole, 134; cooked vegetable salads, 154; Gail's gumbo, 202; hot and sour soup, 204; lentil soup, 205; Middle Eastern slaw, 158; -raisin salad, 152; sautéed parsnips and carrots, 225; shepherd's pie, 111; spicy vegetable soup, 210; -stuffed butternut squash, 220; V-8® vegie soup, 212; vegetable stew, 229

Cashew(s) (also see Glossary — Nuts): butter, 2; cream, 182; curried cashew spread, 5; milk, 17; nutty cookies, 66
Cashew cream, 182: 47; 61; 71; 72; 76; 77; 82; 83; 84; 86; 88; 97; 124
Cashew milk (also see Nut Milk), 17: 47; 51; 54; 60; 61; 187; 192
Cauliflower: broccoli-cauliflower salad, 152; Laurie's broccoli-cauliflower casserole, 98
Celery: baked, 216; blended salad, 151; cooked vegetable salads, 154; hot and sour soup, 204; Middle Eastern slaw, 158; stuffing, 3; V-8® vegie soup, 212
Cereals: 43; 44; 46; 47; 50; 51; 54
Cheese(s) (also see Glossary): Cheddar cheese straws, 3; low-fat "cream cheese," 145; low-fat "sour cream," 145; nutty cheese sauce, 192; pizza supreme, 107
Cherry(ies) (also see Fruit, fresh): fruit and nut turnovers, 33; sauce, 182; -tapioca pudding or pie, 84
Chickpeas (see Beans, garbanzo)
Coconut: blueberry-coconut cream pie, 82; sesame-coconut cream, 185; used throughout
Cookies (see Desserts): 57
Corn (also see Grains; Glossary — Grains): brown rice and corn, 133; bulgur casserole, 134; confetti bean salad, 153; chowder, 199; creamed corn with chives, 221; fresh corn salad, 156; vegetable enchiladas, 127
Cranberry(ies): -nut bread, 32; relish, 183
Crepes: 40
Croutons, 144: 154; 203; 211
Cucumber(s): cold cucumber-yogurt soup, 198; cooked vegetable salads, 154; dressing, 167; gazpacho, 203; mousse, 155; -spinach dip, 4
Dairy substitutes (also see Glossary):
Almond cream, 180
Almond milk, 16
Cashew cream, 182
Cashew milk, 17
Mock "cream cheese," 146
Mock "sour cream," 146
Nut milk, 23
Tofu "ricotta cheese," 148
Dates (also see Fruits, dried): banana-date nut butter, 2; dip or stuffing, 6; -nut cookies, 65; rice, 47; Sama's tea cookies, 69; spicy fruit pancakes, 53
DESSERTS: 57-88
Dips (see Appetizers, Dips and Spreads): 1
Dressings (see Salads and Salad Dressings): 149
Egg replacer (see Glossary)
Endive, Belgian: braised, 217; B R's endive potatoes, 218
ENTREES: 89-128
Fig(s) (also see Fruit, dried): lassi, 18; roll cookies, 66; with cream, 76; whip, 77; spicy fruit pancakes, 53
Flour (also see Glossary): General: roux, 147; whole-grain pancakes, 55

Brown rice: 37; 80
Buckwheat: 46
Cornmeal: 28; 32; 34; 47; 49
Millet: 34
Soy: 35; 37; 65; 68
Wheat, unbleached: 73
Whole wheat: 38; 39; 40; 41; 42; 53
Frozen desserts (see Desserts): 57
Fruit desserts (see Desserts): 57
Fruit, dried (also see individual fruits; Glossary): almond-apricot cheesecake, 81; baked apples, 74; basic granola, 44; fruit-nut balls, 61; fruit platter, 78; Georgian fruit compote, 78; jam, 183; oatmeal-fruit bars, 67; peanut butter-fruit balls, 62; Sama's tea cookies, 69; spicy fruit pancakes, 53; tofu-fruit dip, 12; tropical Waldorf salad, 162; wheatberry cereal, 54
Fruit, fresh (also see individual fruits): apple-tangerine salad, 150; B R's tropical fruit compote, 74; carob-coated fresh fruit, 75; cup, 156; curried fruit dressing, 167; platter, 78; granola-fruit yogurt, 48; papaya with fruit sherbet, 71; pie, 85; smoothies, 19; spicy fruit pancakes, 53; tropical Waldorf salad, 162; wheatberry cereal, 54
Fruit juice concentrate (also see Glossary): fruit soda, 22; used as a sweetener throughout
Fruit juices (also see Beverages):
Mixed: fizzy-fruit punch, 18; fresh fruit smoothies, 19-21; fruit "gello," 77
Apple: 26; 84; 180
Apple-cherry: 70
Apricot: 81
Guava: 18
Peach nectar: 86
Pineapple: 71; 85; 86
Gomasio, 144: 138; 164; 168
Grain(s) (also see Glossary; individual grains): about grains, 130; basic granola, 44; cooking times, 129
GRAIN SIDE DISHES: 129-141
Granola, 44: 4; 48; 79
Grape(s) (also see Fruit, fresh): fresh fruit cup, 156; frozen grapes, bananas and strawberries, 70
Gravy (see Sauces, Savory): 179
Green beans: and red peppers, 223; aspic, 157; confetti bean salad, 153; cooked vegetable salads, 154; French green beans with almonds, 221; oregano, 224; spicy vegetable soup, 210; with water chestnuts, 224; watercress and green bean salad, 164
Greens (kale, turnip or collard): 222
Herbs and spices (see Glossary)
Horseradish: dip, 9; mustard dressing, 172; stuffed beets, 160
Hot taco sauce, 189: 90; 92; 104; 115; 116; 119; 127; 191; 210
Jerusalem artichoke(s): gingered, 223; salad, 158

Kasha (also see Glossary — Grains): about grains, 130; homestyle kasha, 136; -rice cereal, 50
Lentil(s) (also see Glossary — Beans): dried beans, 94; soup, 205; -stuffed cabbage, 100; -vegie loaf, 101
Liquid soy protein (see Glossary)
Low-fat "cream cheese," 145: 3; 4; 6; 221
Low-fat "sour cream," 145: 14; 100; 160; 190; 195; 208; 209; 218
Mango(es) (also see Fruit, fresh): blueberry-mango pudding or pie, 83; fresh fruit pie, 85; ice cream, 71; spicy fruit pancakes, 53
Maple syrup (also see Glossary — Sweeteners): used throughout
Millet (also see Glossary — Grains), 137: about grains, 130; acorn squash with tofu stuffing, 90; muffins, 34; -sesame cereal, 51
MISCELLANEOUS: 143-148
Miso (also see Glossary): dressing I and II, 171; green miso soup, 204; marinated tofu, 102; mock "cream cheese," 146; tofu tetrazzini, 124; sweet and spicy miso gravy, 194
Mock "cream cheese," 146: 3; 4; 6; 221
Mock "sour cream," 146: 14; 100; 108; 190
Muffins (see Breads): 27
Mushrooms(s): barley-mushroom bake, 132; -barley soup, 207; gravy, 191; lemon-ginger tofu, 99; marinated, 10; -potato soup, 208; -rice ring, 138; Russian cabbage pie, 110; -soy pasta sauce, 192; stuffed, 227; tofu-mushroom stroganoff, 120; tofu tetrazzini, 124; zucchini bake, 230
Nut(s) (also see Glossary; individual nuts): basic granola, 44; cinnamon buns, 31; cranberry-nut bread, 32; date-nut cookies, 65; fruit and nut turnovers, 33; -fruit tabouli, 138; ginger-nut waffles, 48; milk, 23; stuffed mushrooms, 227
Nut milk (also see Cashew Milk; Almond Milk), 23: apple milk, 16; apple upside-down cake, 73; banana sauce, 181; blueberry-oatmeal waffles, 45; buckwheat waffles, 46; cinnamon buns, 31; corn chowder, 199; cream of asparagus soup, 200; cream of broccoli soup, 201; kasha-rice cereal, 50; mock "cream cheese," 146; mystery milk, 23; orange-soy muffins, 35; white gazpacho soup, 213; white sauce, 196; whole-grain pancakes, 55; whole wheat crepes, 40
Oatmeal (also see Glossary — Grains): about grains, 130; basic granola, 44; blueberry-oatmeal waffles, 45; carob chip-oatmeal cookies, 64; cinnamon-oatmeal with bananas, 46; -fruit bars, 67; granola pie crust, 79; hardy grain pancakes, 49; nutty cookies, 66; peach cobbler, 86; raisin-spice cookies, 68; Sama's tea cookies, 69; toasted, 54; tofu turkey, 125

Okra: fried, 222; Gail's gumbo, 202; stewed, 227
Orange(s) (see Fruit, fresh)
Pancakes: 49; 53; 55
Papaya(s) (also see Fruit, fresh): 71
Parsnips: 225
Pasta (also see Glossary): lasagna, 98; macaroni garden salad, 137; spaghetti with soy "sausage," 113; tofu-mushroom stroganoff, 120; tofu tetrazzini, 124
Pea(s) (also see Glossary — Beans):
 Chinese peapods: Gail's gumbo, 202; Oriental tofu, 106; summer garden salad, 161;
 Green pea(s): brown rice stuffing, 134; potato-vegetable salad, 159; spicy vegetable soup, 210
 Split pea(s): dried beans, 94; soup, 211
Peach(es) (also see Fruit, fresh): cobbler, 86; fresh fruit cup, 156; granola-fruit yogurt, 48; spicy fruit pancakes, 53
Peanut(s) (also see Glossary — Nuts): butter, 10; spicy peanut sauce, 193
Peanut butter, 10: black walnut balls, 60; carob-peanut butter fudge, 60; cookies, 68; curried tomato dressing, 168; deep-fried bananas, 76; -fruit balls, 62; soup, 208; tofu croquettes, 117; tofu turkey, 125
Pecan(s) (also see Glossary — Nuts): banana-date nut butter, 2; blueberry-oatmeal waffles, 45; nutty cookies, 66; nutty tart shells, 80; plush pecan pie, 87; potato-pecan salad, 159; pralines, 62; stuffed mushrooms, 227; toasted butter pecans, 11
Peppers:
 Chili(es): 8; 189
 Green: used throughout
 Hot (Jalapeño, etc.): 114; 151; 189; 204; 210
 Red: 223
Pie(s) (see Desserts): 57
Pie crust(s) (see Desserts): 58
Pineapple(s) (also see Fruit, fresh): fruit "gello," 77; -strawberry sherbet, 72
Potato(es): B R's endive potatoes, 218; corn chowder, 199; homemade potato chips, 8; homestyle kasha, 136; lentil soup, 205; mushroom-potato soup, 208; -pecan salad, 159; Russian borscht, 209; shepherd's pie, 111; spicy vegetable soup, 210; V-8® vegie soup, 212; -vegetable salad, 159; vegetable stew, 229;
Powdered vegetable broth (see Glossary)
Protein powder, unsweetened (see Glossary)
Pumpkin: 36
Raisin(s) (also see Fruit, dried): carrot-raisin salad, 152; fruit and nut turnovers, 33; -nut bread, 36; sauce, 184; -spice cookies, 68; spicy fruit pancakes, 53
Rice (see Brown Rice)
Roux, 147: 120; 229

SALADS AND SALAD
   DRESSINGS: 149-172
   Dressings: 165-172
   Salads: 137-140; 150-164
SANDWICH COMBINATIONS:
   173-178
Sapodilla: 74
SAUCE(S): 179-196
   Savory: 187-196
   Sweet: 180-186
Seeds (see Glossary): used
   throughout
Sesame (also see Glossary —
   Seeds): -coconut cream, 185;
   gomasio, 144; millet-sesame
   cereal, 51;
Sherbet (see Frozen Desserts): 58
SOUPS: 197-214
Spinach: cucumber-spinach dip,
   4; green miso soup, 204; hot
   and sour soup, 204; individual spinach "quiches," 97;
   lentil soup, 205; nutty
   spinach pie, 105
Spreads (see Appetizers, Dips
   and Spreads): 1
Sprouts (also see Sandwich
   Combinations; Salads;
   Glossary): sautéed bean
   sprouts, 225; watercress-
   sprout salad, 164
Squash:
   Acorn: 90
   Butternut: 220
   Spaghetti: 113; 226
   Yellow: 228; 230
   Zucchini: 214; 230
Strawberry(ies) (also see
   Fruit, fresh): carob-coated
   fresh fruit, 75; frozen
   grapes, bananas and strawberries, 70; fruit and nut
   turnovers, 33; ice cream,
   72; pineapple-strawberry
   sherbet, 72; sauce, 186

Sweet potato: 88
Tahini (also see Glossary): 9;
   96; 171; 195
Tamari (see Glossary): used
   throughout
Tangerine(s) (also see Fruit,
   fresh): 150
Tapioca (also see Glossary —
   Thickening Agents): 84; 86;
   87
Textured vegetable protein
   (also see Glossary):
   Andrea's vegetarian chili,
   91; mushroom-soy pasta
   sauce, 192; rice-stuffed
   cabbage, 108; soy "sausage,"
   112
Tofu (also see Glossary):
   acorn squash with tofu
   stuffing, 90; almond-apricot
   cheesecake, 81; burgers,
   115; carob creme pie, 84;
   creole, 116; croquettes,
   117; -dill dip, 11;
   egg(less) salad I, II and
   III, 118-119; fritters, 119;
   -fruit dip, 12; green miso
   soup, 204; individual
   spinach "quiches," 97;
   kebabs, 120; lemon-ginger,
   99; marinated, 102; mayonnaise, 147; Mexican, 104;
   mock "cream cheese," 146;
   -mushroom stroganoff, 120;
   Oriental, 106; -pineapple
   spread, 12; pizza supreme,
   107; "ricotta cheese," 148;
   roast, 122; scrambled I and
   II, 52; sloppy Joes, 123;
   steak, 123; Szechuan salad,
   114; tetrazzini, 124;
   turkey, 125; -vegetable
   stew, 126; vegetable-
   stuffed, 128; with
   walnuts, 126

Tomato(es): Andrea's vegetarian chili, 91; avocado salad, 150; cabbage-apple soup, 198; catsup, 187; curried tomato dressing, 168; gazpacho, 203; gravy II, 188; green beans oregano, 224; hot taco sauce, 189; Italian tomato sauce, 190; Mexicali dip, 13; Mexican garbanzos, 104; Mexican tomato sauce, 191; mixed bean soup, 206; mushroom-soy pasta sauce, 192; rice, 141; rice-stuffed cabbage, 108; spicy vegetable soup, 210; stewed okra, 227; tofu creole, 116; tofu sloppy Joes, 123; vegetable stew, 229; with basil, 162

VEGETABLE(S) (also see individual vegetables), 215-230: Andrea's vegetarian chili, 91; aspic, 163; cooked vegetable salads, 154; enchiladas, 127; fresh vegetable platter, 6; garden dip, 14; lentil-vegie loaf, 101; raw vegie juices, 24; spicy vegetable soup, 210; -stuffed tofu, 128; Szechuan salad, 114; tofu burgers, 115; tofu kebabs, 120; tofu-vegetable stew, 126; V-8® vegie soup, 212

Vegetable juices (also see Beverages), 15:
Raw vegie: 24
Tomato: 126; 202; 203; 208
V-8®: 157; 212

Vegetable stock (see Glossary): used throughout

Waffles: 43

Walnut(s) (also see Glossary — Nuts): banana-date nut butter, 2; banana-nut biscuits, 29; banana-nut bread, 30; cabbage-walnut sauté, 219; nutty spinach pie, 105; raisin-nut bread, 36; rice-walnut salad, 140

Water chestnuts: green beans with water chestnuts, 224; stuffed mushrooms, 227

Watercress: and green bean salad, 164; cooked vegetable salads, 154; sauce, 195; -sprout salad, 164

Wax beans: 229

Wheatberries (also see Glossary — Grains): 54

Yogurt: cold cucumber-yogurt soup, 198; coleslaw dressing, 165; ginger, 184; granola-fruit, 48; green chili dip, 8; peanut butter soup, 208; sweet lassi, 26

Bibliography

The following publications have either been found to be useful for research or of reference value by the author and members of The G-Jo Institute:

* Baxter, Kathleen M. Come and Get It. Ann Arbor, MI: Children First Press, Box 8008, 1978.

* Bricklin, Mark and Sharon Claessens. The Natural Healing Cookbook. Emmaus, PA: Rodale Press, 1981.

* Callela, John R. Cooking Naturally. Berkeley, CA: and/or Press, 1978.

* Clarke, Christina. Cook with Tofu. New York: Avon Books, 1981.

* Collier, Carole. The Natural, Sugarless Dessert Cookbook. New York: Walker and Co., 1980.

* Davis, Adelle. Let's Cook It Right. New York: New American Library, Inc., 1970.

* Deeming, Sue and Bill. Bean Cookery. Tucson, AZ: H.P. Books, P.O. Box 5367, 1980.

* Doyle, Rodger. The Vegetarian Handbook. New York: Crown Publishers, 1979.

* Echols, Barbara E. Vegetarian Delights. Woodbury, NY: Barron's Educational Series, Inc., 1981.

* Ewald, Ellen B. Recipes for a Small Planet. New York: Ballantine Books, 1973.

* Ford, M. W., S. Hillyard and M. F. Koock. The Deaf Smith Country Cookbook. New York: Macmillan Publishing Co., Inc., 1973.

* Greenberg, K. H. and B. K. Kyte. Versatile Vegetables. San Francisco: Owlswood Productions, Inc., 1355 Market St., 1980.

* Hagler, Louise, ed. The Farm Vegetarian Cookbook. Summertown, IN: The Book Publishing Co., 156 Drakes Ln., 1978.

* Hazelton, Nika. The Unabridged Vegetable Cookbook. New York: M. Evans and Company, Inc., 1976.

* Hewitt, Jean. The New York Times Natural Foods Cookbook. New York: Avon Books, 1971.

* Hills, Hilda C. Good Food, Gluten Free. New Canaan, CT: Keats Publishing, Inc., 1976.

* Hurd, Frank J., D.C., and Rosalie, B.S. Ten Talents. Chisholm, MN: Box 86 A-Route 1, 1968.

* Lappé, Frances M. Diet for a Small Planet. New York: Ballantine Books, 1975.

* Manners, R.A. and Wm. The Quick & Easy Vegetarian Cookbook. New York: M. Evans and Co., Inc., 1978.

* McClure, J. and K. Layne. Cooking for Consciousness. Denver, CO: Ananda Marga Publications, 1976.

* New Age Vegetarian Cookbook. Oceanside, CA: The Rosicrucian Fellowship, 1975.

* Pritikin, Nathan. The Pritikin Permanent Weight-Loss Manual. New York: Bantam Books, Inc. 1982.

* Robertson, L., C. Flinders and B. Godfrey. Laurel's Kitchen. New York: Bantam Books, Inc., 1978.

* Rombauer, I. S. and M. R. Becker. Joy of Cooking. Indianapolis, IN: The Bobbs-Merrill Co., Inc., 1964.

* Shurtleff, Wm. and A. Aoyagi. The Book of Tofu. Kanagawa-Ken, Japan: Autumn Press, Inc., 1975.

* Southey, Paul. The Vegetarian Gourmet Cookbook. New York: Van Nostrand Reinhold Co., 1980.

* Stern, E. and J. Michaels. The Good Heart Diet Cook Book. New York: Ticknor & Fields, 1982.

* Stern, Marina. A Book of Vegetables. Wilton, CT: Lyceum Books, 1978.

* Szilard, P. and J. J. Woo. The Electric Vegetarian. Boulder, CO: Johnson Publishing Co., 1980.

* Thomas, Anna. The Vegetarian Epicure. New York: Vintage Books, 1972.

* Thomas, Anna. The Vegetarian Epicure, Book Two. New York: Alfred A. Knopf, 1978.

* Thrash, Agatha M., M.D. Eat...for Strength. Seale, AL: Yuchi Pines Institute, Route T, P.O. Box 273, 1978.

* What to do with Tofu Cookbooklet, The. Philadelphia, PA: The Grow-cery, 1979.

* Whyte, Karen C. The Original Diet: Raw Vegetarian Guide and Recipes. San Francisco: Troubador Press, 1977.

Colophon

The copy for this book was first entered into a Radio Shack TRS-80 Model II® computer using SCRIPSIT 2.0® software. After a number of printouts and editings, it was finally finished on a Radio Shack Daisy Wheel II® printer, set in Bold PS® typeface. It was then illustrated and delivered to R.R. Donnelley & Sons, Harrisonburg, Virginia, for printing and binding.

It was one of the 14 books written and produced simultaneously, during the spring and summer of 1982, at Falkynor Farm, headquarters of Falkynor Books.

The advent of the micro-computer has radically altered the nature of many things — including that of publishing. Computerized publishing has heralded an "information explosion," bringing with it new challenges in book concept and design. We hope that our answer to those challenges — this book and its relatively unique format — will meet with your approval.